FOR THE BOYS

This 2009 edition published by Metro Books by arrangement with Collectors Press, Inc.

The publisher would like to thank the following: Stephen Fochuk for supplying the majority of vintage nose art photos; Michael Graziolo for his vision and patience in designing this book; Martin Jacobs for supplying several images and helping to create a title; Louis Meisel for his contributions of the patriotic pin-ups; John Campbell and Jeff Endicott for supplying a variety of important images; Brown & Bigelow for their cooperation; the National Air and Space Museum; and the USAF Museum Collection.

The American Airpower Heritage Museum preserves and displays the largest collection of World War II aviation nose art in existence, with thirty-three actual sections of B-17 and B-24 bombers.The AAHM is located on the grounds of the Confederate Air Force Headquarters in Midland, Texas.

Book Design *Drive Comunications, New York*
Project Coordinator *Lisa M. Perry*
Editor *Ann Granning Bennett*
Photographer *Brian McLernen*

Metro Books
122 Fifth Avenue
New York

ISBN: 978-1-4351-2004-4

Printed and bound in Singapore

1 3 5 7 9 10 8 6 4 2

THE RACY PIN-UPS OF WORLD WAR II

FOR THE BOYS

MAX ALLAN COLLINS

METRO BOOKS
NEW YORK

AT YOUR COMMAND!

INTRODUCTION

Starting in 1941 and for the next five years, Bob Hope broadcast his popular weekly radio show from U.S. military bases. Hope—one of the most famous entertainers of the twentieth century and a star in every major medium—remains most renowned for giving something to the boys: variety shows presented on air bases and battleships, at huge camps and obscure outposts, in Alaska and Sicily, England and Africa, for units of the Army, Navy, Air Force, and Marines.

Hope always surrounded himself with a troupe of talented Hollywood and Broadway performers as well as regulars from his radio show. But he also brought the boys a very special gift: at least one pretty girl, a bittersweet reminder of their girlfriends and wives back home.

Singer Frances Langford accompanied Hope on many of the World War II tours. An attractive blonde, Langford once sang "I'm in the Mood for Love" only to have a Seabee shout out, "You've come to the right place, honey!" Hope was glad to admit this line got a bigger laugh than he'd ever got, including when—on stage—Lana Turner said to Hope, "I'm just an ordinary girl," to which Hope replied, "If you're an ordinary girl, I've been going out with soldiers."

Hope was the best known of the stars who traveled to the front lines to entertain, but plenty of other "gypsies" (as Hope called them) were out there giving something back to the boys—Al Jolson, James Cagney, and Ann Sheridan, among many others. And when Glenn Miller toured combat zones with his U.S. Army Air Force Band, he carried a now-forgotten tune, "Peggy, the Pin-Up Girl," in tribute to the numerous examples of nose-cone artwork he'd observed.

Although Navy and Marine regulations largely ruled out the morale-boosting artwork, many Army Air Force units in war zones decorated the noses of their aircraft with vivid cartoonish images that carried American popular culture into foreign skies—wholesome childhood icons like Elmer Fudd, Woody Woodpecker, and Mickey Mouse. More often, however, the subject matter of these enthusiastic amateur artists was a pretty, shapely girl—the epitome of the sweethearts and sirens the boys had left behind.

The idealized girl-next-door mooned over by GIs was largely a Hollywood creation, courtesy of the publicity machines of the major movie studios. Most female stars—even such dignified ones as Barbara Stanwyck, Jean Arthur, and Loretta Young—posed in swimsuits and low-cut gowns in pin-up poses nationally distributed to magazines and newspapers, as well as to various overseas service-oriented publications.

Even MGM's popular Andy Hardy series—the Tinsel Town embodiment of small town values—played the pin-up game. Series entries such as *Andy Hardy's Double Life* (1942), *Andy Hardy's Blonde Trouble* (1944), and *Love Laughs at Andy Hardy* (1946) filled Mickey Rooney's on-screen teenage life with one beautiful starlet after another. Rooney's boyish, gee-whiz, hick-town goofus dated the lovely likes of Lana Turner, Esther Williams, Donna Reed, and Kathryn Grayson. It must have rubbed off on the real-life Rooney, who famously—and disastrously—married Ava Gardner in 1942.

GIVE TO USO UNITED SERVICE ORGANIZATIONS

And the ex-Mrs. Rooney (a.k.a., the ex-Mrs. Artie Shaw and the ex-Mrs. Frank Sinatra) provides us a good a place as any to begin taking a brief, if longing, look at some of the major Hollywood pin-up queens.

Born in Smithfield, North Carolina, in 1922, Ava Gardner (her real name) suffered an unhappy childhood followed by storybook success: in New York seeking secretarial work, Ava got her photo snapped, which lead in 1940 to a Hollywood contract at MGM. During the war years, she landed numerous showy bit parts and supporting roles, including the ingénue *In Ghosts on the Loose* (1943) with the East Side Kids. She is a prime example of an actress whose fame was boosted by her stunning pin-ups, to postwar fame as the femme fatale who doomed boxer Burt Lancaster in *The Killers* (1946).

A major movie love-goddess of the late 1940s and 1950s, Gardner starred in such box-office favorites as *One Touch of Venus* (1948), *Showboat* (1951), *Mogambo* (1953), and as Clark Gable's love interest in a steamy remake of *Red Dust*, which had originally starred 1930s sex symbol Jean Harlow. The woman once described as "the most beautiful animal in the world" evolved into a fine character actress in films such as *On the Beach* (1959), *Night of the Iguana* (1964), and *Seven Days in May* (1964). She died in 1990.

Another sultry brunette whose postwar star was shaped by wartime pin-ups was Ernestine Jane Geraldine Russell. Born in 1921 in Bemidji, Minnesota, in the heart of dairy country, Russell set a standard for bosomy beauty that reverberated throughout the 1950s. Eighteen-year-old Jane Russell—a sometime model, full-time receptionist, and would-be actress—posed for photos that somehow got into the hands of Howard Hughes. The legendary eccentric business mogul, dashing aviator, and renegade movie-studio chief hired Russell to portray Rio in his Billy the Kid epic, *The Outlaw*.

After firing Howard Hawks—one of the great directors of Golden Age Hollywood—Hughes took over the direction of the western himself, right down to the design of a cantilevered brassiere for his amply endowed teenage leading lady. Russell's low-cut dresses—for a role that required plenty of bending over—made *The Outlaw* a soldier's dream and a censor's nightmare. Shot in 1941, *The Outlaw* was withheld for three years, during which time Hughes dispensed pin-ups of Russell reclining in a haystack, overflowing her low-cut peasant blouse. One of the most famous pin-up images of all time (the painted movie poster was the work of top calendar artist Zoë Mozert), Russell's bosomy haystack lounging was a prime subject of nose-cone artists.

Withheld by Hughes from any other film roles during those war years when her pin-ups were making her famous, Russell became one of the most popular glamour girls of the 1950s. In particular, she made her mark as a comedienne, notably in the Bob Hope vehicle *The Paleface* (1948) and its sequel *Son of Paleface* (1952), and in *Gentlemen Prefer Blondes* (1953), in which she good naturedly shared the screen with sensational love goddess Marilyn Monroe. By the early 1970s, Russell's career on the big screen was over, replaced by touring-company stage work and a successful stint as a TV pitchwoman for bras (for "full-figured gals").

A notorious film was key in the career of another of Hollywood's most exotic beauties, Hedy Lamarr (born Hedwig Eva Maria Kessler). Born in 1913 in Vienna, Austria, Lamarr began making German and Austrian films in 1930. One of them, *Ecstasy* (1933), included a nude swimming sequence followed by a startling orgasmic love scene, which made the stunning brunette an international sensation. Her role opposite Charles Boyer in *Algiers* (1938) ushered in her mysterious persona, perhaps best exemplified by her performance as Tondelayo in *White Cargo* (1942).

Hardly a girl-next-door, Lamarr represented a mysterious, exotic, yet accessible brand of sexuality that made her one of the most appealing wartime pin-up girls. The Cecil B. De Mille epic *Samson and Delilah* (1949) revealed a woman at the apex of her allure. She retired from the screen in 1958, her radiance undiminished. Lamarr claimed that "any girl can be glamorous: all you have to do is stand still and look stupid"; but she belied this wry commentary with breathtaking natural beauty and an intellect that included inventing (with film composer Antheil) a radio-control device for torpedoes. Developed during World War II, it did not go into use until 1962 and is still used as an anti-jamming device in satellite communications.

Of the exotic beauties, however, the most popular among GIs was Dorothy Lamour. Born Mary Leta Dorothy Kaumeyer in December 1914, in New Orleans, Louisana, Lamour was voted one of the GIs top five favorite pin-up girls in a well-publicized wartime survey. Lamour became famous as "the Sarong girl," ably filling out that scrap of a garment and reigning as Paramount's (and Hollywood's) most popular South Seas maiden. From 1936 until after the war, the barely clad Lamour struck striking poses in moonlight-washed jungle settings and sang lovely songs well.

But Lamour's appeal to GIs was more than her exotic good looks and shapely figure. Because Dorothy was a talented singer and comedienne willing to spoof her sarong-clad self (notably in the classic Bob Hope/Bing Crosby *Road* series), and because she was equally at ease and credible as a contemporary woman in modern dress, she rose to a greater, more enduring fame than rival South Seas sirens Maria Montez and Yvonne DeCarlo. Though her career floundered after the war, with the exception of the occasional *Road* picture, Lamour deftly extracted nostalgic value from her wartime popularity with road show musicals and big-band revival appearances. She died in 1996.

Lamour's rival island queens—the aforementioned Montez and DeCarlo—may not have made the GI top five, but their sexy images graced many a barracks and foxhole.

Born Maria de Santo Silas in the Dominican Republic in 1918, Montez was a 1940s sensation at Universal Pictures, her shapely, sultry brunette charms enhancing the likes of *Arabian Nights* (1942) and *Ali Baba and the Forty Thieves* (1943). "When I see myself on the screen," she once said, "I am so beautiful I jump for joy." Many GIs had a similar reaction. But by her sadly premature death by heart attack in 1951, her film career was waning.

That other mysterious screen beauty—the future Mrs. Herman Munster, Yvonne DeCarlo—was a native not of some exotic island, but Vancouver, British Columbia. Born Peggy Yvonne Middleton in September 1922, DeCarlo had been a dancer since childhood when, as a teenager, she won the "Miss Venice Beach," title and the breathtaking brunette beauty was soon stripping in Los Angeles nightclubs. By 1942, she was in the movies, alternating between playing harem girls and dancehall queens. In addition to "The Munsters" TV series (1964-1966), DeCarlo, like Lamour, took to the stage, notably in her Broadway turn in Stephen Sondheim's "Follies."

Despite the popularity of these island vixens, the wholesome, milk-fed blondes of Hollywood were the top favorites of homesick GIs. Although both Jane Russell and Dorothy Lamour were in the top five of favorite pin-up girls, the list was well-rounded out by Betty Grable, Lana Turner, and Rita Hayworth.

Hayworth was a strawberry blonde (and starred in the 1941 Warner Brothers film of that name), and the tempestuousness of many of her roles linked her to the sultry approach of Lamarr, Lamour, Montez, and DeCarlo. But Hayworth's popularity eclipsed those harem girls, in part because she was perceived as more talented. Lovely as she was, Hayworth's gifts were greatly enhanced by Hollywood slight-of-hand: her singing voice was dubbed, cropped shots of fancy footwork were not always of her, and even a hand model filled in for close-up work.

Nevertheless, pin-up expert Steve Sullivan has termed Hayworth "the unsurpassed Love Goddess" of Hollywood's Golden Age and regards her famous *Life* magazine cover—in which Hayworth is perched on her knees on a bed with a look that is at once knowing and innocent—"the era's most utterly glamorous photo." Sullivan, editor of the definitive pin-up magazine, *Glamour Girls: Then and Now*, also deems Hayworth "the greatest pin-up of World War II, her image inflaming the dreams of millions of GIs," citing the fact that Hayworth's nose-cone image even adorned the atomic bomb dropped, appropriately, on the island of Bikini.

Brooklyn girl Hayworth, born Margarita Carmen Cansino in October 1918, performed with her family's vaudeville act ("I had castanets in my hands instead of rattles," she once said). She made an inauspicious film debut in a Vitaphone short as part of the Dancing Cansinos at age eight—already a seasoned veteran. A few years later, her Spanish-born father, Eduardo, exploited his teenage daughter's burgeoning beauty in seductive dance routines that caught the attention of a Fox Film executive. Rita was only seventeen when she danced in the Spencer Tracy film *Dante's Inferno* (1935).

Hayworth's breakthrough came with the Howard Hawks classic, *Only Angels Have Wings*. At age twenty-one, Rita was acting opposite Cary Grant, and her sexy, sultry image was cemented with her siren role opposite Tyrone Power in *Blood and Sand* (1941). Dancing with Fred Astaire and Gene Kelly in wartime musicals kept her in the spotlight, but it was her semi-striptease ("Put the Blame on Mame, Boys") in *Gilda* (1946) that defined her screen image for all time. Stormy high-profile marriages to Orson Welles, Aly Khan, and Dick Haymes only added to her screen image as a temptress. Her last significant role was opposite Frank Sinatra in *Pal Joey* (1957), and she died in 1980 after a tragic, all-too-public decline from Alzheimer's disease.

"Sweater girl" Lana Turner, born Julia Mildred Frances Turner in Idaho in February of 1921, was still a high-school girl when (as legend would have it, anyway) she was spotted in Schwab's Drugstore on Hollywood's Sunset Boulevard. As a sexy, tightly-sweatered schoolgirl, she pranced down the street in *They Won't Forget* (1937) and instantly won the hearts of schoolboys who would soon be GIs.

Although Turner's image was definitely girl-next-door in her early career, her definitive performance was undoubtedly that of the murderous Cora in the 1946 taboo-bursting *The Postman Always Rings Twice* (from James M. Cain's seminal crime novel). Never has an actress dressed in white so convincingly portrayed the evil at the heart of all-American darkness. The girl-next-door Turner evolved into one of the most sophisticated women of 1950s cinema, starting with the lurid *Peyton Place* (1957), from the controversial Grace Metalious best seller. Big-screen soap opera-ish melodrama became Turner's forte, echoed by events in her own life—her gangster boyfriend Johnny Stompanato was knifed to death by Turner's teenage daughter Cheryl. The all-American sweater girl, so beloved by GIs in the 1940s, became a slightly fallen if not still glamorous symbol of the disappointments of life in the post-war world.

The undisputed queen of the wartime pin-up girls was Betty Grable, born Ruth Elizabeth Grable in December 1916 in St. Louis, Missouri. Grable described herself as "strictly an enlisted man's girl." A great musical comedy star, Grable—whose peaches-and-cream beauty personified the American girl-next-door—was only thirteen when she appeared as a show-girl in *Whoopee* (1930), the Samuel Goldwyn film of Eddie Cantor's great Broadway success. The scene-stealing starlet attracted major attention in *Du Barry was a Lady* (1939) and *Down Argentine Way* (1940). During the war years, her cheerful musicals—including *Moon Over Miami* (1941), *Springtime in the Rockies* (1942), *Coney Island* (1943), and *Pin-Up Girl* (1944)—were just the confections to soothe both the boys overseas and their families on the home front.

Unlike Rita Hayworth—Grable's only major competition for the number-one spot as pin-up girl of the era—Betty did her own singing and dancing. Her shapely legs were insured by Lloyd's of London for more than a million dollars. At the time married to famed trumpeter/bandleader Harry James, Grable posed for her famous leggy rear-view pin-up—the single most famous pin-up image of World War II—when she was many months pregnant.

Grable graciously handed the blonde sex-queen mantle over to her *How to Marry a Millionaire* (1953) co-star Marilyn Monroe, stepping down from the screen after making *How to be Very, Very Popular* (1955), ironically a film Monroe refused to do. Grable was successful as a nightclub star and toured in *Hello Dolly* in the 1960s. She died in July 1973.

Hayworth, Turner, and Grable were not the only blonde goddesses worshipped by nostalgic fighting men. Betty Hutton, a less glamorous Grable, was a gifted comedienne who brought her bouncy, somewhat screwball style to the likes of *The Fleet's In* (1942) and *Star-Spangled Rhythm* (1942). Her exaggerated manner was out of fashion by the mid-1950s, however, and after some successful public appearances at major venues such as New York's Palace and the London Palladium and several well-received nightclub engagements, the gifted Hutton slipped into an unfortunate obscurity, fueled by her failure to succeed in the new medium of television.

Veronica Lake, petite, shapely, famed for her peek-a-boo eye-obscuring hair style, was one of the most popular wartime leading ladies, making a big impression in the jingo-istic *I Wanted Wings* (1941); Preston Sturges's comic master-piece *Sullivan's Travels* (1941); and the precursor to TV's

"Bewitched" series, *I Married a Witch* (1942). Frequently paired with equally diminutive leading man Alan Ladd in crime classics such as Graham Greene's *This Gun for Hire* (1942), Dashiell Hammett's *The Glass Key* (1942), and Raymond Chandler's *The Blue Dahlia* (1946), Lake had a sultry quality more often associated with brunettes such as Lamarr, Lamour, and Lauren Bacall (nicknamed "The Face" and a pin-up favorite herself).

The beautiful actresses of Hollywood popularized not only by their films but the studio publicity machines—enjoyed a symbiotic relationship with the great pin-up calendar artists of the day. Just as the artists drew upon clip files of photographic pin-ups from magazines and newspapers, the actresses and those who shaped their images were influenced by the idealizations of American beauties as filtered through the artistry of George Petty, Alberto Vargas, Earl Moran, Gil Elvgren, Earl MacPherson, and a legion of other "girlie" artists.

Robust commercial artist George Petty (1894-1975) began a series of color cartoons for *Esquire* in the early 1930s that featured gorgeous girls and their unlikely, un-handsome suitors. Gags were provided by another of the seminal men's magazine's top cartoonists, E. Simms Campbell, himself no slouch when it came to drawing pretty girls. Soon the beauties, with their dazzling smiles and sleek-as-a-Buick curves, held solo center stage, and the Petty Girl was born.

The classy if risqué venue of *Esquire* gave the pin-up respectability, and Petty's amazing airbrush technique put him at the forefront of commercial artists. Petty and his namesake pin-up girl became household words. He landed such major advertising accounts as Old Gold cigarettes (who issued the first Petty pin-up calendar), Springmaid sheets, and Jantzen swimsuits and foundations. His pin-up-style rendering of Rita Hayworth even graced the cover of *Time* magazine (November 10, 1941). But his *Esquire* pay rate did not keep pace with his popularity, and, in the early 1940s, he bolted *Esquire* in a money dispute, replaced by (the also underpaid) Alberto Vargas.

Post-*Esquire*, Petty painted calendar girls for *True* magazine (1945-48) and, finally, a long-running series for the evocatively named Rigid Tools. He also did a notable series of covers for the program booklet of the traveling "Ice Capades" show. In the 1950 Hollywood film *The Petty Girl*, the rotund artist was portrayed by slim Robert Cummings, and "The Petty Girl" herself was more accurately depicted by Joan Caulfield, with an entire calendar brought to life by twelve lovely models. (Earlier, Petty had provided a stunning series of pin-ups for the 1946 musical *Ziegfeld Follies*.)

For many, the Petty Girl remains the ultimate pin-up, a canny combination of pseudo-realism and fantasy. With their oversize heads, impossibly tilting breasts, defined musculature, heavy legs, and archly positioned hands and feet (the latter, in later years, frequently ensconced in ballet slippers), Petty's girls hardly embodied the standards of female beauty of the various eras the artist worked in. Yet his flawless technique, its sheen as seductive as a new-car showroom, allowed him to deliver his personal vision of pulchritude in a manner so irresistible his audience never seemed to notice it didn't match their own.

Petty, who studied art in Paris before World War I, lived a Hemingway-esque lifestyle, hunting big-game in Africa. His daughter Marjorie, his primary model, described him as a "perfectionist" who often spent ten days on a single painting. Shortly before his death, Petty finally buried the hatchet and drew one last Petty girl for *Esquire*; though her figure had not changed, her hair had turned a dignified gray, and granny glasses perched on a pert nose.

His name has become synonymous with pin-up girls, but in the early 1940s, Peruvian Alberto Vargas (1896-1982) was just a guy hired by *Esquire* magazine to imitate Petty. Vargas initially aped Petty's sleek women with their telephone posing and large-hat lounging, even down to the Petty-like cartoon touches (phones and hats drawn in with red crayon.) Gag lines were replaced with mildly racy poetry. Soon, however, Vargas's distinctive, delicate watercolor style emerged, and his pin-up girls became more voluptuous and distinct than his predecessors'. Nearly as unreal as Petty's, the Vargas Girl seemed more grounded in reality, an impossible dream with at least some chance of coming true. These wide-eyed, wasp-waisted wonder women rivaled Hayworth and Grable as the ultimate World War II pin-up girl.

Vargas, who signed his *Esquire* work with the slightly less ethnic "Varga", had already achieved some notoriety for his *Ziegfeld Follies* and movie-poster art. But *Esquire* (and its yearly calendars) made him famous, though he was poorly paid and wretchedly overworked. Like Petty, he eventually quit, but legal problems over ownership of his work—even when he used his own signature when he marketed his own calendar and playing-card sets in the late 1940s—plagued him.

Like Petty, Vargas found a second home at *True* magazine, where lovely pin-ups were accompanied by photos of the artist and his models at work (one of them was famed TV "Sheena" Irish McCalla). Similar layouts appeared in *Modern Man*, and Vargas never entirely disappeared from the scene. An occasional movie poster appeared—the 1951 RKO feature *Behave Yourself* had Shelley Winters posing—but by the mid-1950s, Vargas was painting "legacy nudes" for his beloved wife Anna to sell after his death.

In 1957, however, Vargas was given a second shot at fame and fortune by longtime fan Hugh Hefner, an ironic salvation considering Hefner's *Playboy*, with its lush photographic nudes, had largely put the purveyors of painted pin-ups out of business. Vargas's regular *Playboy* slot through the 1960s and 1970s elevated the artist to a pinnacle that eclipsed even Petty himself.

Vargas lived to see his work achieve a fame and financial success that virtually made him the Norman Rockwell of pin-up artists. Like George Petty, Vargas had his own quirky vision of feminine beauty; unlike Petty, Vargas could impart an individuality to his women—and perhaps that was ultimately the biggest difference between these two giants: Petty painted girls, Vargas painted women.

In 1939, Merlin Enabnit was hailed by *Life* magazine as England's answer to George Petty. The Merlin Girl was a favorite of British "Tommys" (GIs) via regular appearances in *Sketch* magazine, but American soldiers also enjoyed Merlin's sleek, airbrushed damsels, who certainly invoke Petty, right down to the trademark telephone posing and preening, although they have their own bounce and personality.

Postcards, magazine covers, and a campaign for White Owl cigars attempted to make "the British Petty" a hit in the States, but his fame never approached his rival's level. Still, Merlin was a hugely successful commercial illustrator in the U.S. market, his beaming, curvaceous, yet graceful beauties adorning ads for soda pop, beer, soap, undergarments, and automobiles, among many other items.

Merlin bristled at being called a "disciple" of Petty, whom he never met, and, although his mastery of airbrush rivaled his better-known peer, Enabnit worked his pin-up magic not just in airbrush but in straight watercolor as well as pastels, acrylic, and oils. Like Vargas, Merlin created more distinct girls (and women) than Petty, whose pin-ups basked in a constant bright light. Merlin lavished the curves of his beauties with patterns of light and shadow that were more revealing than their form-fitting sunsuits.

Ironically, Merlin was not British. He was born near Des Moines, Iowa, in 1903, and worked out of Chicago, with time out for a mid-1940s Hollywood stint, where his models included dancer Vera Ellen and actress Virginia Mayo. He later earned greater fame in America than his pin-ups had brought him by painting a series of portraits of United Nations luminaries, among others.

A handsome, dapper six-footer, Merlin, like so many pin-up artists, occasionally posed for photographs with his fetching models. Even after abandoning pin-up art (his granddaughter quoted Merlin as saying he'd decided this pursuit was an unworthy application of his gift), Merlin was a "celebrity" artist, making guest appearances on television shows and presenting painting workshops that attracted broad media attention.

The artist was well known enough for a "Merlin Enabnit's No. 1 Palette Knife" to be marketed nationally (with such techniques, he could turn out a finished landscape in several hours), and he authored four how-to books for Walter Foster on subjects including painting with a palette knife, portraiture, and the use of color. He was perhaps best noted for his color sense (authoring a hardcover book, *Nature's Color Concept*, in 1975) than for his fabulous pin-ups and skillful portraiture.

Still, when he became one of the few Americans to be granted the title "Fellow of the Royal Society of Arts" by the Queen of England, those girls the Tommys took to their hearts, and with them into combat, must have played a role.

The father of the American pin-up, Rolf Armstrong (1889-1960) came to fame in the 1920s, an era his romantic, drowsily sensual females seem to typify. Armstrong's expert, confident use of the pastel medium spawned famous followers such as Billy DeVorss, Earl Moran, and Zoë Mozert, and his approach itself (if not his favored medium) was a clear influence on Alberto Vargas, Gil Elvgren, and Merlin Enabnit.

Armstrong did many covers for magazines and song sheets (all highly collectible now) and was perhaps best known for his close-up portraits of dreamily sensuous Clara Bow-ish "It" girls, who seemed to emerge from a brilliant swirl of some single vivid color, often red. His nonspecific backgrounds, from which a very specific girl emanated, became a convention followed by countless others.

The popularity of his sultry close-ups aside, it was the artist's dazzlingly smiling, flowingly maned, supple-limbed calendar girls for Brown & Bigelow that set the glamour-art standard. Michigan-born Armstrong, who studied at the School of the Art Institute of Chicago, also contributed covers to magazines such as *College Humor*, *Life*, and *Shrine* and his commercial accounts included Oneida Silverware.

With a pastel palate of 3,600 colors, Armstrong worked from live models in his Manhattan studio, creating enormous originals typically sized 28 by 39 inches, surviving examples of which are among today's most valuable pin-ups. A one-time pro boxer and devoted seaman, ruggedly handsome Armstrong was rarely seen without his yachting cap and enjoyed promoting both a man's-man persona and (in numerous photo layouts) the fantasy life of an artist surrounded by beautiful models.

Next to the *deco* dolls of George Petty, his immediate successor as "Pin-Up King," and the painterly yet commercial-illustration Haddon-Sundblom style of Gil Elvgren, Armstrong's *art-nouveau* style seemed quaint even during much of his own lifetime. Unlike Vargas, who had similar artistic roots, Armstrong's girls with their bee-stung lips and heavily shadowed, hooded bedroom eyes, always seemed to be children of the 1920s, even when alive with flapperish glee. By the mid-1940s, when his stint with Brown & Bigelow was winding down, Armstrong's work seemed hopelessly dated, though in recent years a reassessment has rightly restored him to the pantheon.

The most famous female pin-up artist, Zoë Mozert (1907-1993), is an exemplary disciple of the Rolf Armstrong pastel style. Often her own model, Mozert is noted for rejecting sexy-girl clichés in favor of depicting more real-seeming young women with recognizably individual features and personalities.

Her cover portraits of Hollywood starlets for publications such as *Romantic Movie Stories* and *Screen Book* were particularly popular, but she also contributed covers to such diverse periodicals as *American Weekly* and *True Confessions*. Although the bulk of her work was calendar-oriented (primarily for Brown & Bigelow), Mozert also made a mark as a movie-poster artist, notably with Carole Lombard's *True Confession*, and, of course, the previously mentioned, notorious Jane Russell/Howard Hughes sex-and-sagebrush saga, *The Outlaw*. Even

Mozert's less sultry sirens exude both charm and sex appeal, sending the girl-next-door signals the boys overseas so enjoyed.

At first glance, Billy DeVorss might be dismissed as a shameless imitator of Rolf Armstrong, whose influence extended even to DeVorss's signature. A native of St. Joseph, Missouri, DeVorss worked out of New York's Greenwich Village from the mid-1930s until his early 1950s return to the Midwest with his earliest calendar girls appearing under the Louis F. Dow imprint. Like Armstrong, the largely self-trained DeVorss used live models, worked in pastels, and his beauties often displayed dazzling smiles and sleek limbs.

But DeVorss had his own special charm. His works, while uneven, have a warmth and glow, and his girls-next-door radiate a good natured sexuality. Where Armstrong conveyed glamour, DeVorss conveyed romance. His idealized women seem to benefit from his lack of formal training. Perhaps it's no coincidence that his favorite model was his wife.

In recent years, Gillette A. Elvgren (1915-1980) has joined the rarefied ranks of Petty and Vargas as a premiere American pin-up artist. His exquisite oils of gorgeous girls next door—their skirts often blowing up to reveal lovely silk-clad limbs—rival his mentor Haddon Sundblom's Coca-Cola Santas for sheer nostalgic pleasure. Working in Sundblom's shop with Al Buell and Andrew Loomis (among other noted illustrators), Elvgren contributed to various Coca-Cola ads himself. Legendary illustrator Sundblom, who had studied at the American Academy of Fine Art, taught his star pupil the lush brushstroke technique that made Elvgren's girls such glowing wonders.

Elvgren created deco-ish pin-ups for publisher Louis F. Dow from the late 1930s into the 1940s, and it was these images that were so widely circulated to servicemen during World War II. His long postwar run with calendar company Brown & Bigelow sealed his fame, and he became the premier chronicler of postwar pulchritude. Today, his oils on stretched canvas, which measure 24 by 30 inches, are second in value only to originals by Vargas.

Earl Moran (1893-1984) was a master of pastels, though he showed little if any influence by reigning Brown & Bigelow star Rolf Armstrong, whose domain he encroached upon in the 1930s. Iowa-born and a School of the Art Institute of Chicago student, prolific Moran was soon a superstar, creating lively, sexy girls whose relationship with the viewer was seldom a teasing one. Unlike Elvgren and others, Moran did not continually rework any one type of situation, and his pin-ups have more variety than any other major contributor to the field.

Breaking in via advertising work for Sears Roebuck, Moran went on to magazine illustration (*Life*), movie posters (*Something For the Boys*, 1944), and even co-published an early "girlie" magazine, *Beauty Parade*, for which he contributed covers (sometimes under his middle-name *nom de plume*, "Steffa"). His most enduring pin-ups feature his famous late-1940s model Marilyn Monroe. Later he turned to oils and, working from the late-1950s until his death, an outstanding series of sensual nudes.

One of the most successful and imitated of pin-up artists, Earl MacPherson (born in Oklahoma in 1910) originated the famous "Artist's Sketchbook" series for Brown & Bigelow, in which a central, finished figure is augmented by rough side sketches. World War II service interrupted his B & B work, although the calendar company reprinted his calendars numerous times, and these images were among servicemen's most popular pin-ups. During this period, K.O. Munson became the first of his many successors. After the war, Mac signed with Shaw-Barton for a similar successful series.

Mac worked with live models, and men's magazine spreads of him painting lovely nudes scattered about his modernistic Southern California studio further added to his renown. The versatile MacPherson, who died in 1993, also earned a considerable reputation as a western artist.

These were the superstars of the pin-up world. But like the enlisted men who won the battles, numerous lesser-known, yet glowing lights, added their talents to the pin-up war effort. Here is some background on some of the artists whose work appears in this book.

Jules Erbit, master of pastels, was one of the most prolific pin-up artists from the 1930s to the 1950s. His lovely women graced calendars, posters, and prints published by C. Moss and others. Erbit typifies the glamour approach: a typical Erbit pin-up features a lovely woman in a gown leaning against the rail of a ship or lounging in a garden. It's a soft-focus, flowers-in-the-hair world. The artist's masterful use of pastels for his radiant beauties puts him securely in the camp of Rolf Armstrong followers. But unlike Billy DeVorss, Erbit has his own immediately recognizable style. Where Erbit most resembles Armstrong is in the size of the few known surviving originals: massive works, they typically measure 31 by 41 inches.

The bold, outrageously fetishistic pin-ups of Peter Driben are often "keyhole" glimpses of faintly S&M-oriented imagery, leaning on loony lingerie, fishnet stockings, and spike heels. Cover artist for the Bob Harrison stable of girlie magazines, Driben depicted voluptuous, leggy dames who, in their eye-popping outfits, have a sense of humor that keeps the dark side of fetishism at bay; their appearances in *Beauty Parade, Eyeful, Flirt, Titter, Whisper,* and *Wink* make those magazines highly collectible even when Betty Page isn't a featured model. Driben was painting portraits of Palm Beach socialites at the time of his death in the late 1970s.

Walt Otto created beaming American beauties in lushly painted oils on canvas. Despite their Elvgren-style romantic realism, Otto's paintings contain cartoonier elements, particularly in the expressions of his winsome girls (as well as his cartoonist's-style signature). Additionally, his women are less coy than Elvgren's: an Otto girl, typically attired in short shorts or a swimsuit and occasionally tugged along by a cute mutt or two, stares unabashedly at the viewer.

D'Ancona's painterly style, lush brushstrokes, warm colors, and girl-next-door beauty of his subjects suggest a close linkage to Elvgren and Sundblom. A prolific contributor of calendar-girl art to numerous companies, D'Ancona's earliest works appear to have been for Louis F. Dow. These are stiff, even awkward pin-ups. Later, an improved D'Ancona landed advertising accounts, including several soft-drink firms that capitalized on his Sundblom-like style, so identified with Coca-Cola.

Albert Leslie Buell, a paperback cover artist and magazine illustrator, worked with Elvgren in the Sundblom shop in Chicago. His oils are among the best pin-ups in that medium, although existing originals (on board, not canvas) are much smaller than those of Elvgren. Perhaps that explains a certain delicacy in his work; Buell's pretty girls really are "pretty." These girls-next-door are captured in typically girlish pursuits of the time, such as sewing, playing tennis, or swinging in a swing. Underclad as they are, Buell's girls have a wholesome ingenuousness rare in the pin-up form.

One of the handful of major female pin-up artists, Pearl Frush worked in watercolor, although it's not always apparent in the published versions of her works. Fairly prolific from the wartime 1940s into the 1950s, Frush produced fresh, shapely pin-up girls who share with Mozert women an individuality and reality the men in the field seldom achieved. Her originals are comparatively tiny (typically 14 by 19 inches) and reveal a delicate, flawless technique as beautiful as her subjects. She may be Vargas's only true rival in watercolor.

Versatile Art Frahm—yet another Chicago area artist and a likely Sundblom-shop graduate—often presented his girls-next-door as perfectly coifed, daring decolletage-dressed beauties aglow in the midst of romantic soft-focus settings. But Frahm also excelled in (and perhaps created) the campily sexist "embarrassment" series for publisher A. Fox, in which a lovely girl is literally caught with her panties down, her lacy undies slipping to her ankles while she's in the process of bowling, walking the dog, or changing a tire.

I PAY NO MORE THAN TOP LEGAL PRICES
I ACCEPT NO RATIONED GOODS WITHOUT GIVING UP RATION STAMPS

When Earl MacPherson entered the service, K.O. Munson was drafted from the Brown & Bigelow stable to take over the successful "Artist's Sketchbook" series. Sticking to the pastel medium, Munson replaced MacPherson's Petty-smooth pin-ups with sharper, crisper lines, though the soft curves of his bright-eyed beauties were definitely appealing. Soft-spoken sportsman Munson had been (and continued to be) a successful commercial artist, and over the years his clients included Lucky Strike, Goodyear, Motorola, U.S. Rubber, Mars Candy, and Sealy Mattress (an ad for the latter featured a fetching Munson beauty lounging on a cloud). Moving from Chicago to St. Paul in 1936, Munson was a top Brown & Bigelow pin-up artist throughout the 1940s, spending the 1950s back in Chicago, where he opened his own studio and continued to create pretty-girl art for various companies.

Hollywood and commercial illustration weren't the only sources for the dream-girls-next-door of the World War II GI. American fighting men had not long before been boys who grew up on the great comic strips of the 1930s. Two of their favorite cartoonists noted for fashioning fantastic funny-page females provided pin-up inspiration.

Al Capp's Li'l Abner—considered by many (including this writer) to be the greatest comic strip of all time—was noted for its unique combination of hillbilly slapstick and sophisticated satire. More pertinent to the boys overseas were the scantily clad Dogpatch "gals" including Daisy Mae, the voluptuous blonde who pursued hapless hillbilly Abner at every Sadie Hawkins' Day (eventually catching him in the postwar world). Daisy and the lovely but malodorous Moonbeam McSwine joined the girls of Petty, Vargas, and company as frequent subject matter for nose-cone art.

Capp provided occasional comics to the war effort—particularly on the homefront—while his friend Milton Caniff served up a pin-up-oriented strip (free of charge) for servicemen. Caniff's popular newspaper strip "Terry And The Pirates"—with its bevy of beauties including Burma, Normandie Drake, and the legendary Dragon Lady, as well as its Asian locale—had been one of several strips ("Joe Palooka" among them) that had run storylines from around 1939 on dealing with the coming war. After Pearl Harbor, Terry Lee, the boy hero of the strip, grew up quickly and joined the U.S. Army Air Force, and Caniff—whose canny view of world politics made the federal government suspicious that military insiders were leaking information to the cartoonist—turned his exotic adventure strip into a war story.

Caniff contributed "Male Call" to the U.S. Department of War's Camp Newspaper Service. He initially used the sexy blonde Burma from "Terry", but soon shifted to a new character, Miss Lace, the number-one comic-strip pin-up girl of all time.

"I didn't base Lace on any movie stars," Caniff said. "She was the visualization of an idea...a wish fulfillment for the readers....The whole thing was the point of view of the American GI, the American guy suddenly dumped in a place he'd never heard of before. What he's really thinking about is the girl back home, not the tavern wench near the air base in England."

Raven-tressed Miss Lace, whom Caniff viewed as "innocent but sexy as hell," probably appeared on more nose cones than any movie star or recycled Vargas, Petty, or Elvgren image.

Miss Lace—a creation so famous she rivaled the Dragon Lady herself—was Caniff's contribution, the way he found to give something to the boys. "Male Call" was discontinued shortly after the war, and Caniff considered Lace a creature of that specific time, that specific war. There was no need for a pen-and-ink fantasy once the boys had gone home to embrace the girls who were now women and who would soon be mothers. Miss Lace, like the Petty girl, and Betty Grable, had promised a wonderful postwar world, but real girls-next-door would keep that promise.

We hope you enjoy this scrapbook of pin-up memorabilia that indicates just how popular, how essential to the war effort, these sweetly sexy images were, proving that if you really want to give something to the boys...send in the girls.

MAX ALLAN COLLINS

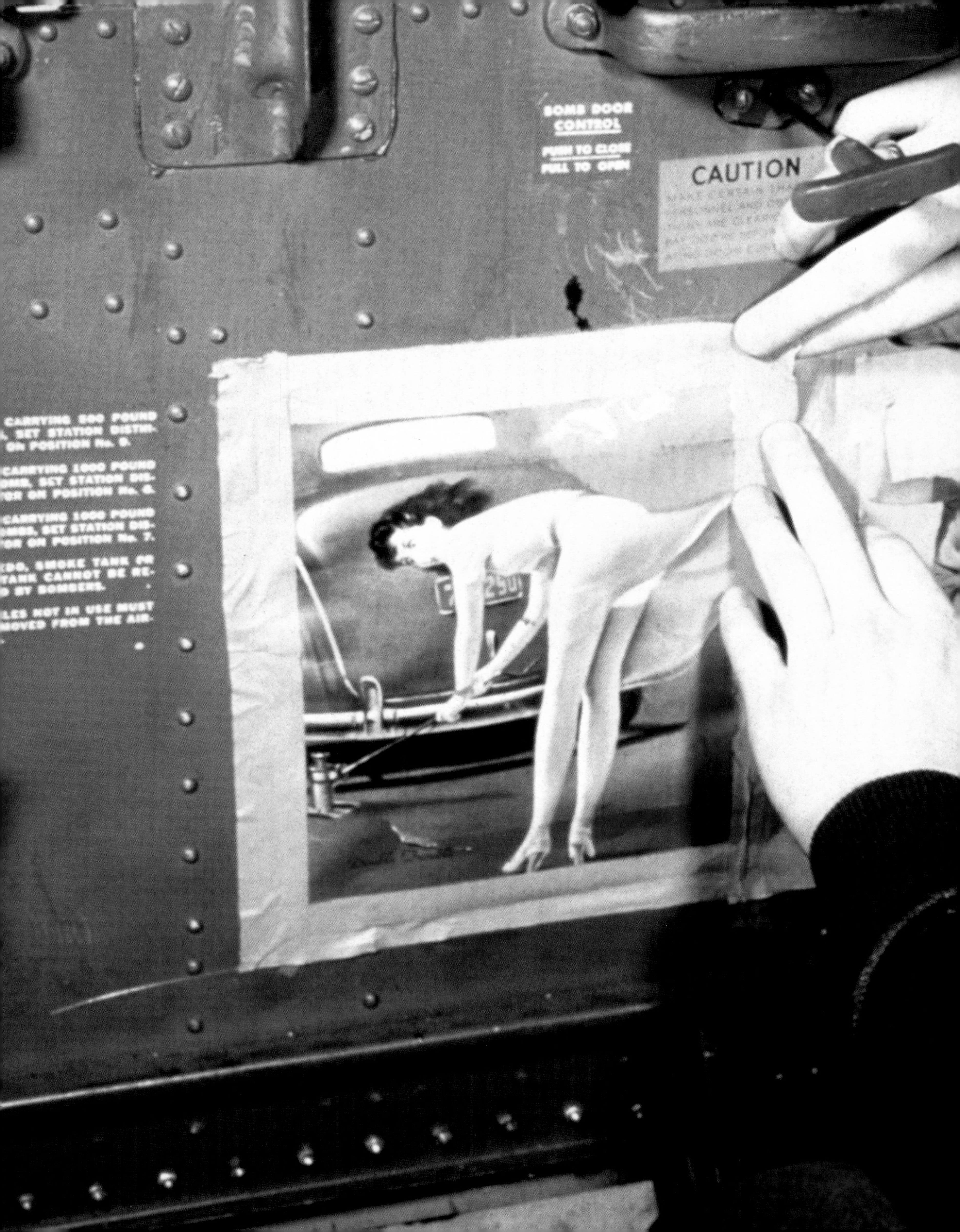

BOMB DOOR
CONTROL
PUSH TO CLOSE
PULL TO OPEN
CAUTION

BEAUTIFUL MEMORIES

The glorified pin-up girls of artists like Gil Elvgren were pinned (and sometimes taped) where the boys serving their country could get a pleasant reminder of what they were fighting for. The innocence of the homefront settings of these pin-ups make a poignant contrast to the combat zones where they were frequently seen.

STATION WOW
ELVGREN

Boeing B-29 "Super Fortress" 'Victory Girl'

North American B-25 "Mitchell"

Lockheed P-38 Lightning

North American B-25 "Mitchell"

Consolidated B-24 "Liberator"

Republic P-47 "Thunderbolt"

Consolidated B-24 "Liberator"
'Kentucky Belle'

Consolidated PB4Y-2

North American B-25 "Mitchell"

North American B-25 "Mitchell"

North American B-25 "Mitchell"

Every BOND You BUY Puts A PLANE in the SKY
Buy WAR BONDS
BUD'S LUNCH
SHORT AND SWEET!
NOB GRILL
In Downtown Portland
12th & Washington
Exclusive
But Not Expensive
Quality Food
Myrna & Bill Halpin
Young dog- Old trick!
EL GAUCHO TAVERN
Beer and Mixers
To Take Out
HENRY'S CAFE
A PLACE FOR FRIENDS TO MEET & EAT
Hank & Chris Groleau
Props.
13148 E. Valley Blvd.
Basset, Calif.
PHONE ED. 6-9001
ANYONE FOR TENNIS?
PARA-CUTIE
NEELS RESOR
WE HAVE IT
ANYTHING ON TONIGHT?
ON EVERY FLIGHT
Delicious
Chiclets
Refreshing
JACK POT CAFE
Cold Beer
Al & Eunice Gamble
Props.
Phone 9181
Farmington, Calif.
YOU ARE ALWAYS WELCOME
IN PERFECT SHAPE!
McCLOSKEY VARNISH CO.
VARNISHES - SYNTHETICS
SURFACE COATINGS
PHILADELPHIA
CHICAGO
VARKYDS - VARKOLS
A TWO-GUN GAL!
SUNSET INN
Beer & Wine
HAMBURGERS
Phone 101-J-3
A BATON BEAUTY
LOG FRONT TAVERN
4433 N.E. Union
Portland, Ore.
Phone TR. 0312
Always a friendly WELCOME
SITTIN' PRETTY
STRICTLY FOR THE "SEE"!
Your Favorite SPOT
UNITED WE STAND
"POOL"
I WANT 2 CUBA
CUSTOMER OF MINE
I TREAT YOU RIGHT!
Bramble Inn
BAR-B-Q
WE FEATURE
FRENCH FRIES
TASTY
SANDWICHES
PR. 4-9437
6738 S.E. 52nd Ave.
PORTLAND
IN PERFECT SHAPE!
Maid in Baltimore
CLOSE COVER FOR SAFETY
ROBBINS INN
Lois & Jack Downing
Phone MU. 9651
3000
N. Commercial Ave.
Portland 12, Oregon
Always a friendly WELCOME
Maid to Order!
KEEP 'EM ROL
CLEAN SWEEP
HE SAYS, HE'S AFRAID HE'LL DIE!
Young and Kittenish!
HUDSON'S
Richfield Service
Lubrication - Tune-Up
& Wheel Balancing
LI. 6731
12208 N.E. HALSEY
PORTLAND, OREGON
PRIDE OF THE HAREM
WE HAVE IT
GROCERY
PUTTING ON THE DOG

STRIKE IT UP

Matchbooks made a perfect—if diminutive—home for many a pin-up girl, warming males overseas and on the home front. Many of these images are by Earl MacPherson and his assistant, T.N. Thompson.

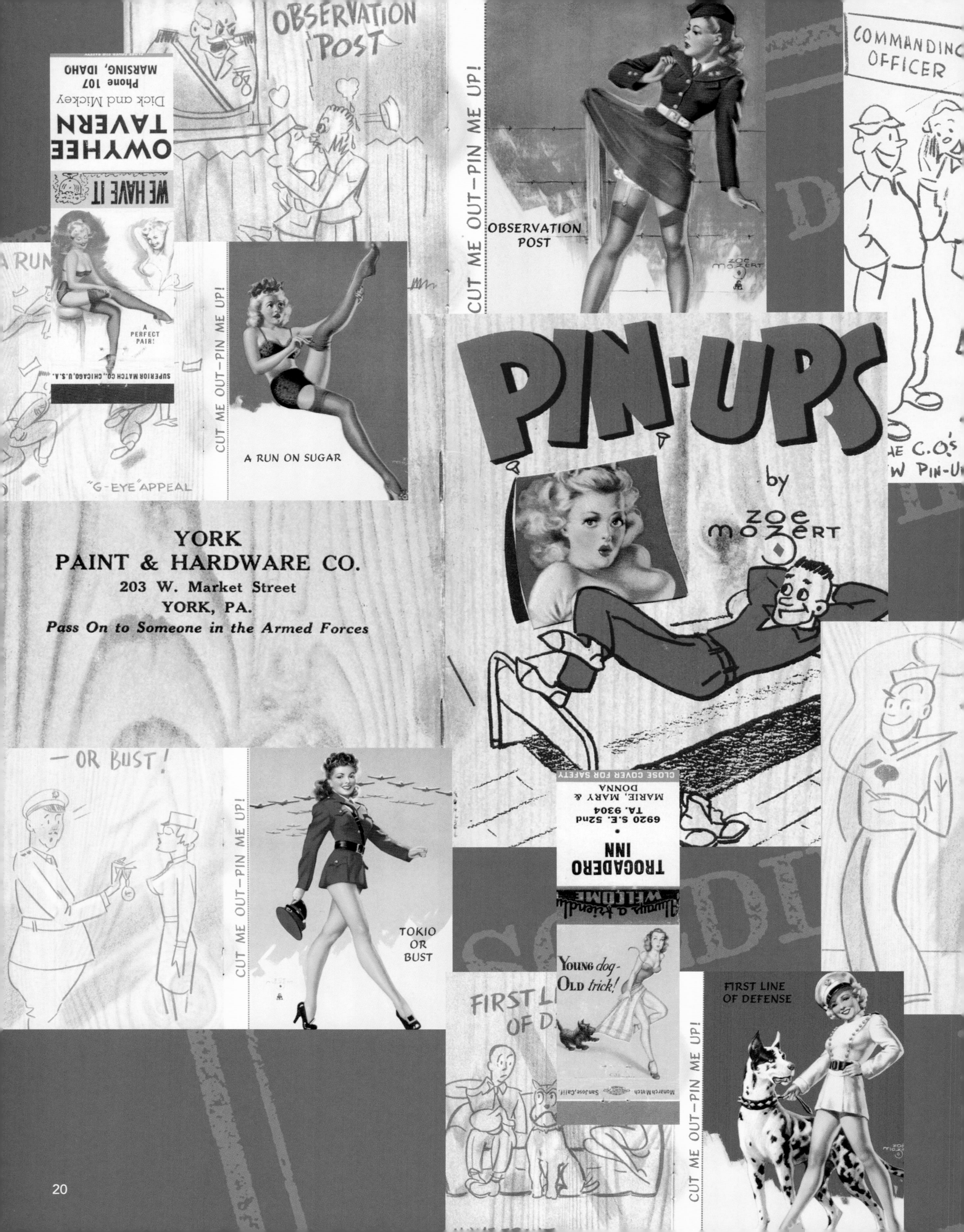
OBSERVATION POST
WE HAVE IT
OWYHEE TAVERN
Dick and Mickey
Phone 107
MARSING, IDAHO
A PERFECT PAIR!
SUPERIOR MATCH CO., CHICAGO, U.S.A.
CUT ME OUT—PIN ME UP!
A RUN ON SUGAR
"G-EYE" APPEAL
CUT ME OUT—PIN ME UP!
OBSERVATION POST
COMMANDING OFFICER
PIN-UPS
by
ZOE MOZERT
YORK
PAINT & HARDWARE CO.
203 W. Market Street
YORK, PA.
Pass On to Someone in the Armed Forces
— OR BUST!
CUT ME OUT—PIN ME UP!
TOKIO OR BUST
CLOSE COVER FOR SAFETY
MARIE, MARY & DONNA
TA. 9304
6920 S.E. 52nd
TROCADERO INN
WELCOME
Young dog-
Old trick!
Monarch Match
San Jose, Calif.
FIRST L
OF D
CUT ME OUT—PIN ME UP!
FIRST LINE OF DEFENSE

CUT ME OUT–PIN ME UP!
HIT THE DECK
NOB GRILL
NEW · CLEAN · GOOD EATS
BR · 9031
NOB GRILL
In Downtown Portland
12th & WASHINGTON
EXCLUSIVE
BUT NOT EXPENSIVE
PARA-CUTIE
CUT ME OUT–PIN
CHUTE THE WORKS
TRUE BLUE PIN-UP
FOR THE GUY WHO'S MARRIED OR ABOUT TO BE
SHOW THE
ME OUT–PIN ME UP–VISITOR'S DAY
WORK LIKE A HORSE?
CUT ME OUT–PIN ME UP!
CUT ME OUT–PIN ME UP!
PURSUIT TYPE
CUT ME OUT–PIN ME UP!

Consolidated B-24 "Liberator" 'Slip Stream'

“What legs they had though! It’s all in fun and this is what makes a lot of us forget when the war is going to end.”

AUGUST 9, 1945

North American B-25 "Mitchell" 'Sherry'

Consolidated B-24 "Liberator" 'Lilas Marie The 2nd'

Consolidated B-24 "Liberator" 'Nancy'

North American B-25 "Mitchell" 'Betty Grable'

"M-my sister, Sir—She's the affectionate type."

COPR. 1944 EX. SUP. CO., CHGO., MADE IN U.S.A.

Boeing B-29 "Super Fortress" 'Rose Marie'

Martin Marauder B-26 'Mary Ann'

Louise
Mary
ELVGREN
CLOSE COVER BEFORE STRIKING
OREGON GOLD COAST
Brighton, Ore.
Hiway 101
FINE FOODS
TED'S PLACE
TO HAVE A FRIEND
be one
DO-IT-YOURSELF
KID

SPORT MODEL

Consolidated B-24 "Liberator" 'Louise Mary'

Consolidated B-24 "Liberator" 'Net Results'

Boeing B-17 "Flying Fortress" 'Little Patches'

VICTOR TCHETCHET

May 1945

Sunday	Monday	Tuesday	Wednesday	Thursday	Friday	Saturday
		1	2	3	4	5
6	7	8	9	10	11	12
13 Mother's Day	14	15	16	17	18	19
20	21	22	23	24	25	26
27	28 Memorial Day	29	30	31		

Plenty on
the Ball
WINTER'S LOVELY QUEEN

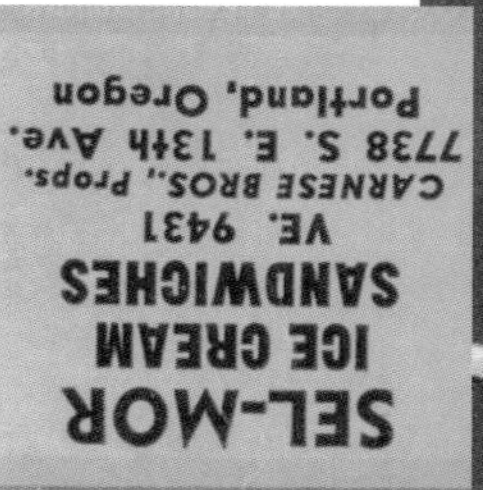

A KNOCKOUT

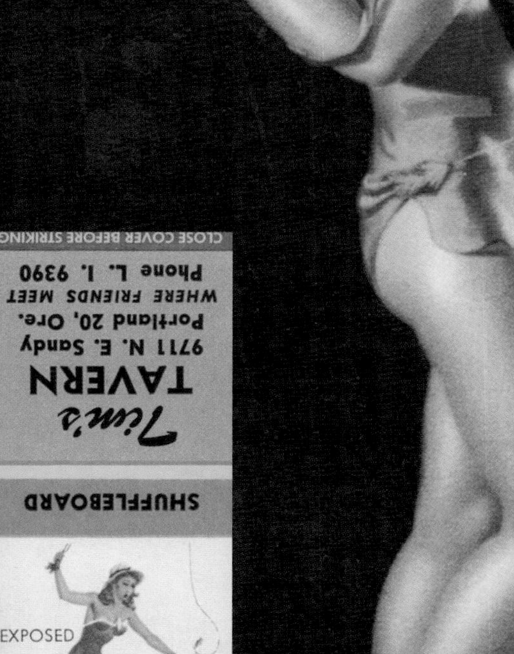

A GOOD CATCH

Republic P-47 "Thunderbolt" 'Bottoms Up'

"Next time your medals drop down here, I'm going to keep them!"

Boeing B-29 "Super Fortress" 'Constant Nymph'

Boeing B-29 "Super Fortress"
'Forbidden Fruit'

Boeing B-17 "Flying Fortress"
'Mount'N Ride'

Consolidated B-24 "Liberator" 'Shoo-Shoo Baby'

Boeing B-29 "Super Fortress"
'Untouchable'

Boeing B-29 "Super Fortress"
'Cream of the Crop'

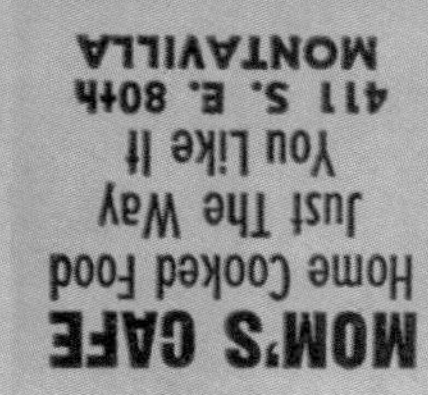

Consolidated B-24 "Liberator"
'Well Developed'

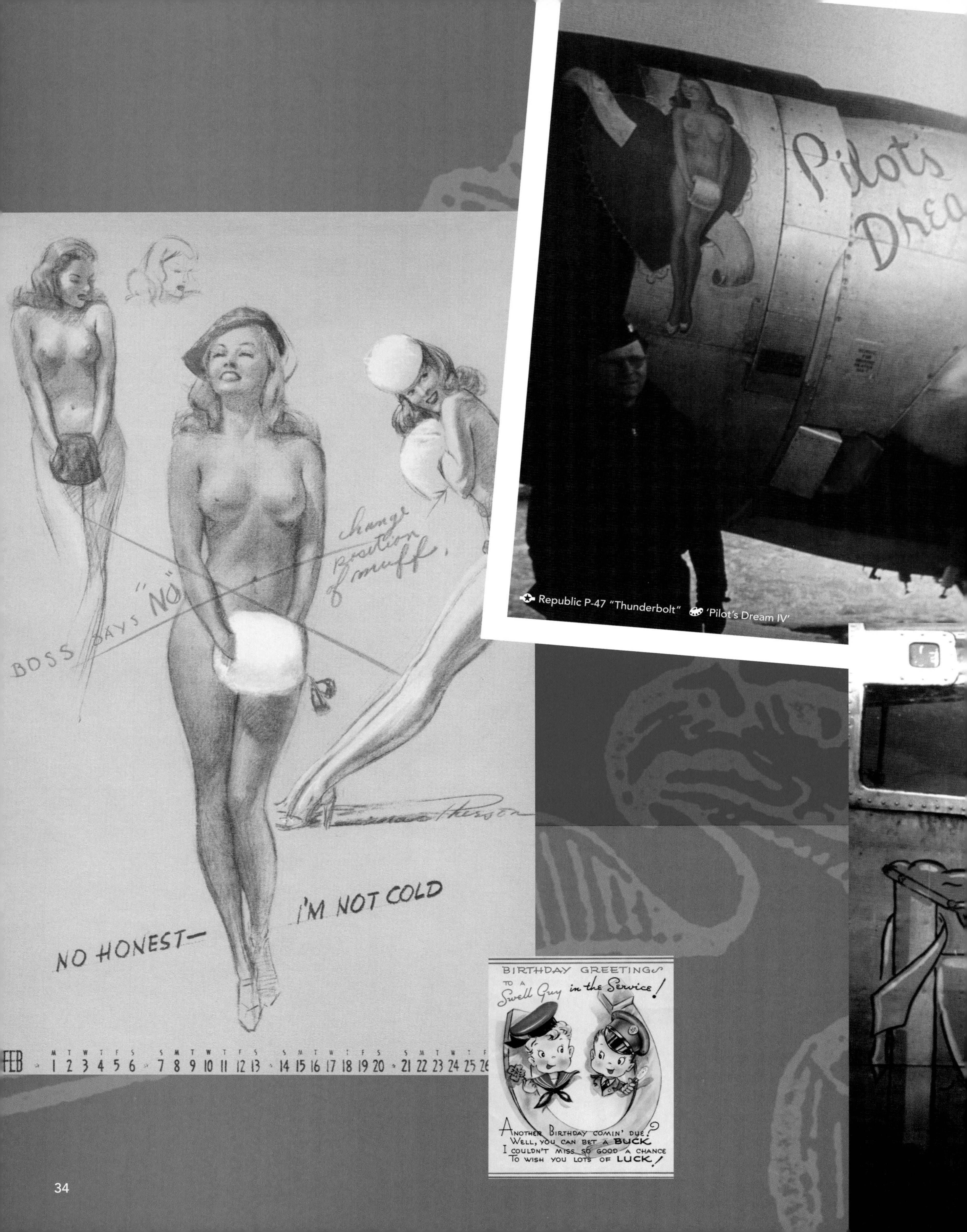

Republic P-47 "Thunderbolt" 'Pilot's Dream IV'

North American B-25 "Mitchell"

I'M EXERCISING MY RIGHTS— AND LEFTS!

Boeing B-29 "Super Fortress"
'Million Dollar Baby'

BUY
WAR BONDS
EVERYBODY
EVERY PAYDAY
AT LEAST 10%

LIBERTY

7TH
WAR LOAN
Pace Press, Inc., New York, N. Y. 3-1-45-12¾MM. Key 734

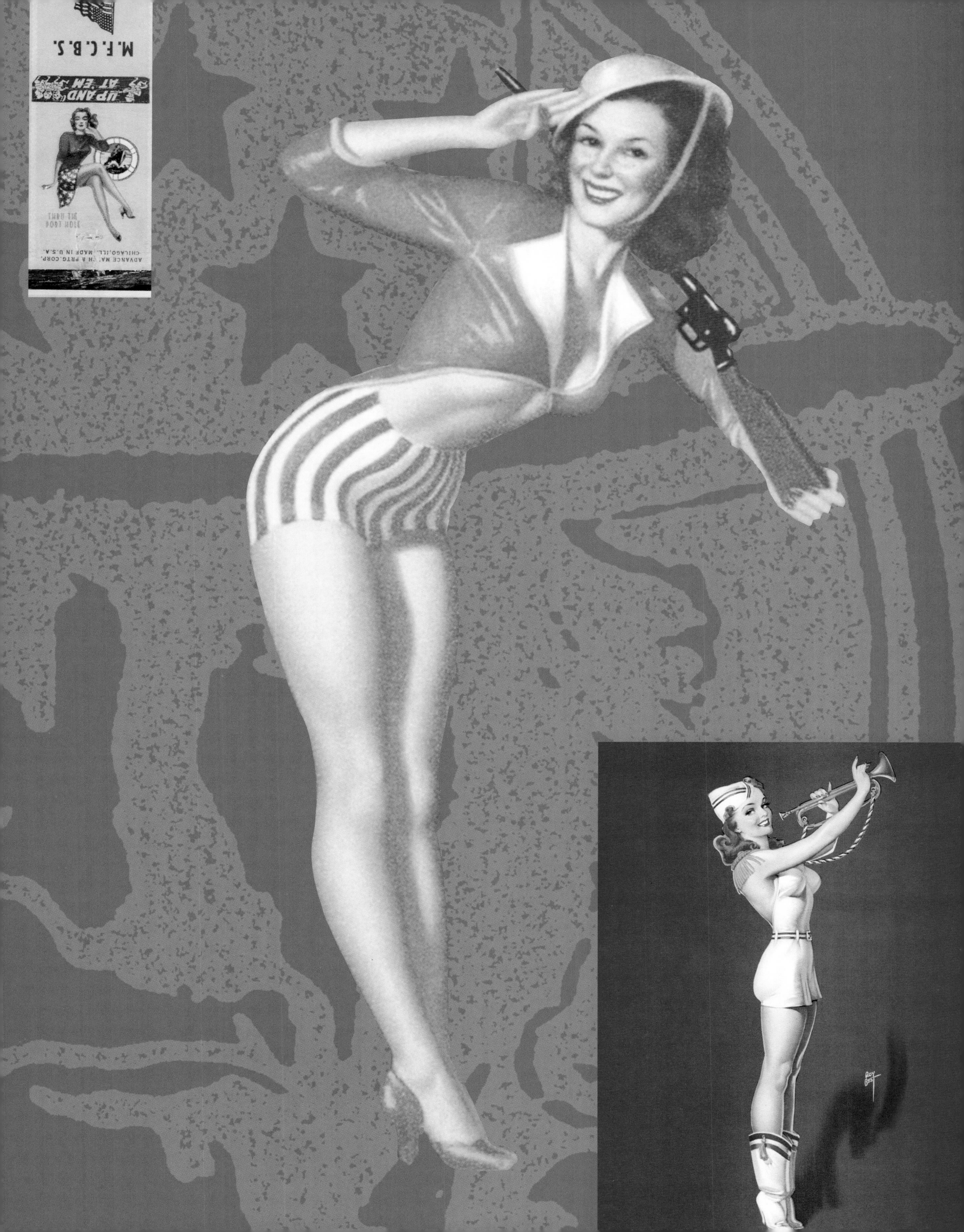
M.F.C.B.S.
UP AND AT 'EM
THRU THE PORT HOLE
ADVANCE MATCH & PRTG. CORP.
CHICAGO, ILL. MADE IN U.S.A.
ROY BEST

Boeing B-29 "Super Fortress"
'Pride of the Yankees'

Consolidated B-24 "Liberator" 'Shady Lady'

Boeing B-29 "Super Fortress"
'Arise My Love and Come With Me'

Lockheed P-38 F-5 Lightning 'Ginger Snap'

Lockheed P-38 Lightning 'Sleepy-Time Gal'

Consolidated B-24 "Liberator" 'Night Mission'

Consolidated B-24 "Liberator" 'Sack Time'

MALE CALL

As Milton Caniff's famous wartime comic strip punningly invoked it, mail call was a precious time of day for G.I.s. Sexy and/or amusing stateside art enlivened many a letter or postcard sent overseas.

70th
SEABEES
BATTALION

Marianas Islands
Sunday 17 June

Good Evening

Many thanks for the thought on June 6th.

Work has slowed down somewhat in the unit and many of our evenings are either spent out on the ball field or in some other entertainment sector.

Played softball last Sunday against the Medical Dept. The yeomen took a beating and most of us were "bushed" from the ordeal. The breakfast the following morning and succeeding mornings did not

Boeing B-29 "Super Fortress" 'Pacific Queen'

Boeing B-29 "Super Fortress" 'Sky Queen'

Boeing B-29 "Super Fortress"
'Coral Queen'

Consolidated B-24 "Liberator"
'The Duchess'

Consolidated B-24 "Liberator" 'Queen Mae'

Consolidated B-24 "Liberator"

Consolidated B-24 "Liberator" 'Photo Queen'

“Hawaiian music is heard often on the islands but it is true that ‘G.I. Jane’ prevails. It is a surprise to hear Bing Crosby and others during the day!”

DECEMBER 1, 1944

Boeing B-17 "Flying Fortress"
'Little Miss Mischief'

Boeing B-29 "Super Fortress" 'Little Gem'

Boeing B-29 "Super Fortress"
'Little Gem'

IT'S JUST A STEP
OVER THE BORDER
EB 1 2 3 4 5 6 7 8 9 10 11 12 13 14 15 16 17 18
CLOSE COVER FOR SAFETY
JACKSONVILLE, CAL.
Hwy. 120 & 49
FISHING SUPPLIES
AND INFO.
KLEIN'S
Eats - Drinks
Grocery
MOTEL - GAS & OIL
AN ORCHID
FOR BETSY
Monarch Match San Jose, Cal.
ARTIST'S
SKETCH
KEEP YOUR POWDER HIGH!
AUG 1 2 3 4 5 6 7 8 9 10 11 12 13 14 15 16 17 18 19 20 21 22 23 24 25 26 27 28 29
23 24 25
WE'RE PROUD OF
OUR "E"QUIPMENT, TOO
HERE COMES THAT HIGH PRESSURE DIVER AGAIN

WHAT'S COOKIN'?
MENU
I FEEL—
A LITTLE BIT BACKWARD
NOW WATCH MY JINGLE JANGLE JINGLE
HUDSON'S
Richfield Service
Lubrication - Tune-Up
& Wheel Balancing
12208 N. E. HALSEY
LI. 6731
PORTLAND, OREGON
Washing and Greasing
PRIDE OF THE HAREM
CAN YOU TIE THESE?
— THERE WAS
THE MAMA BEAR..
THE PAPA BEAR..
AND WOO-WOO!

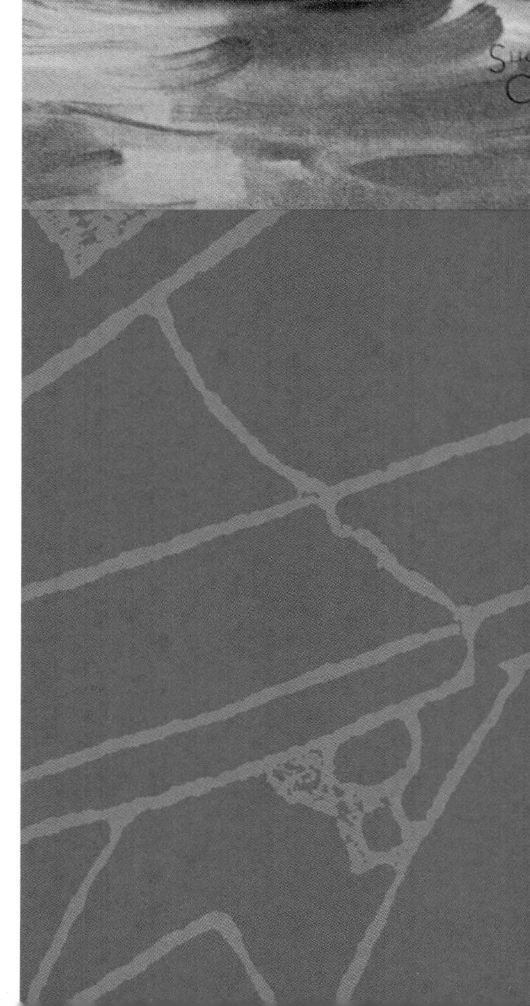

Consolidated B-24 "Liberator" 'Lonesome Lady'

Consolidated B-24 "Liberator" 'Innocent A–Broad'

DOUBLE EXPOSURE

Consolidated B-24 "Liberator" 'Hay Maker'

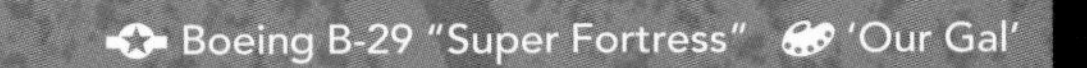
Boeing B-29 "Super Fortress" 'Our Gal'

Boeing B-29 "Super Fortress" 'Our Baby'

Republic P-47 "Thunderbolt" 'Drink'n Sister'

Boeing B-17 "Flying Fortress" 'Our Gal Sal'

Consolidated B-24 "Liberator" 'Dangerous Critter'

Boeing B-17 "Flying Fortress" 'Knockout Dropper'

Boeing B-29 "Super Fortress" 'Tokyo Twister'

Consolidated B-24 "Liberator" 'Liquidator'

Consolidated B-24 "Liberator" 'The Rip Snorter'

WILD CARDS

Playing cards have traditionally made an ideal home for lovely pin-ups. This array includes images by Gil Elvgren, Joyce Ballantyne, Earl MacPherson, and Zoë Mozert (among others).

HIT THE DECK
FRED PETERS
Indiana Avenue
PLAYING CARD CO.
CHICAGO
MADE IN U.S.A.
H.M.S. EXCELLENT
Player's

A.A.A.A.
FIRE EXTINGUISHER
SERVICE
NO JOB
TOO LARGE
OR TOO SMALL
OUTSIDE CHANCE
MATCH CORP. OF AMERICA • CHICAGO.
MADE IN U.S.A.
Open Till 4 A.M.
PUTTING ON THE DOG
KOTHS SPEC. VANCOUVER, WASH.
MADE IN U.S.A.
CLOSE COVER FOR SAFETY
BLUE BELL
TAVERN
ANGIE
DAVE
DOUG
615 W. Burnside St.
Portland 9, Oregon
BR. 8364
Just a Little DIFFERENT
Young and Kittenish!
Monarch Match San Jose, Calif.
LET'S GET TOGETHER
EV & MURPH'S
Pool
Snooker
LADIES WELCOME
TEMPTATION
Universal Match Corp., Portland
"Made in the West for the West"
Art Frahm
CUTE TRICK

Bird's Eye View

ELVGREN

ANKLES AWEIGH

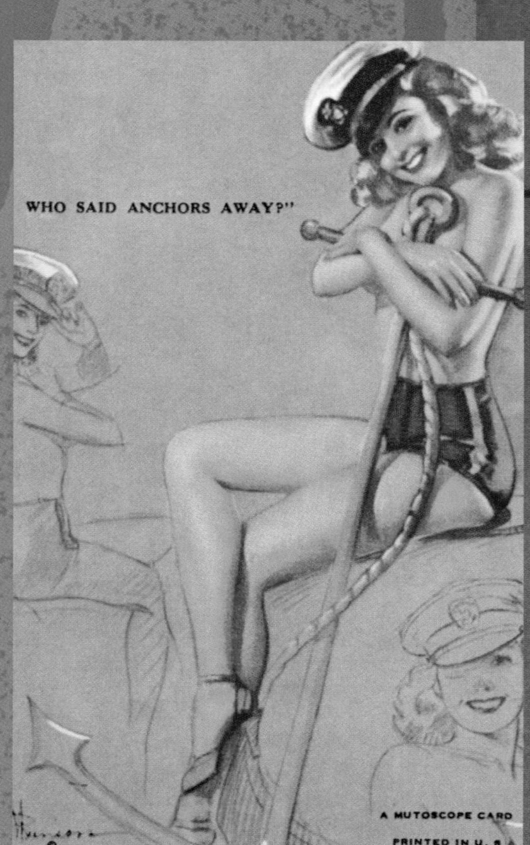

Open Till 4 A.M.
BIGGEST LITTLE STORE IN TOWN
CITY GROCERY
1735 S. W. BROADWAY
PORTLAND 1, ORE.
BR-0818
SHAPING UP
Hi Ya, Sailor! Bet this is the Longest Letter You ever got!
PETER DRIBEN

Sun	Mon	Tue	Wed	Thu	Fri	Sat
	1	2	3	4	5	6
7	8	9	10	11	12	13
14	15	16	17	18	19	20
21	22	23	24	25	26	27
28	29	30	31			

YOU ARE ALWAYS WELCOME

SNOW DADDY!

Monarch Match San Jose, Calif.

Ship Shape

YOUR ADVERTISEMENT
IN THREE OR FOUR LINES
WILL MAKE FRIENDS
ALL THE YEAR

SUN	MON	TUE	WED	THU	FRI	SAT
*	*	*	*	1	2	3
4	5	6	7	8	9	10
11	12	13	14	15	16	17
18	19	20	21	22	23	24
25	26	27	28	*	*	*

JOE ROSSBACK

You'll be **sitting pretty** with Quality Park Products on di
Leatheroid wallets with their natural good looks and wide
sizes will sell themselves—with **Repeat Sales!**

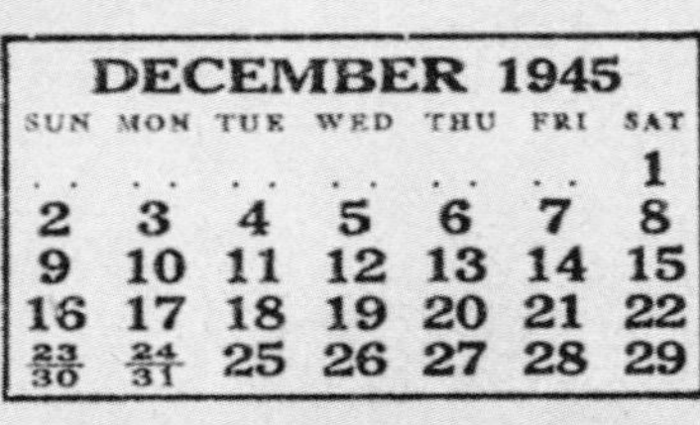

ST. PAUL 4 450 N. Syndicate Street NEstor 18
CHICAGO 6 564 W. Monroe Street CENtral 31

DECEMBER 1945

SUN	MON	TUE	WED	THU	FRI	SAT
						1
2	3	4	5	6	7	8
9	10	11	12	13	14	15
16	17	18	19	20	21	22
23/30	24/31	25	26	27	28	29

Pin-Ups
12
GORGEOUS
GLAMOUR
GIRLS
Each print is securely bound yet will tear out with a nice clean edge for Pin-Up or framing.
★
Easily mailed to any part of the world for
(3rd class).
nailed under
(1st class)
en in foreign
. Convenient
attached to
FAITHFUL REPRODUCTIONS
of
ORIGINAL PAINTINGS
NCH DRESSING
ER SERIES TO FOLLOW . . . WATC

"Wouldn't I make a good petty officer?"
Greetings from
G. M. PEARSE & CO.
965 Broad Street
NEWARK 2 :: NEW JERSEY
MY SISTERS AND I CAN HELP YOU WITH YOUR PROBLEMS (Turn Me Over)

SERIES THREE ★ ★ ★
PIN-UPS
12 GORGEOUS GLAMOUR GIRLS
FAITHFUL REPRODUCTIONS OF ORIGINAL PAINTINGS
ELVGREN
Each print is securely bound, yet will tear out with a nice clean edge for Pin-Up or framing.
Easily mailed to any part of the world for 3c postage (3rd class). Must be mailed under 12c postage (1st Class) to Army men in foreign countries. Convenient self-mailer attached to back cover.
A LIVE WIRE
OTHER SERIES TO FOLLOW • WATCH FOR THEM!

NO
PARKING
"I got a little behind in my rent."
Greetings from
G. M. PEARSE & CO.
965 Broad Street
NEWARK 2 :: NEW JERSEY

“There is always plenty to do. There’s a movie on now. These keep one *quite* interested. Hedy Lamarr is featured tonight.”

APRIL 30, 1945

Consolidated B-24 "Liberator"
'Lady From Hades'

'Lady from Hades' bomber jacket

'Target for Tonight' bomber jacket

Consolidated B-24 "Liberator" 'Gremlins Delight'

Boeing B-17 "Flying Fortress"
'Naughty Nancy'

Republic P-47 "Thunderbolt"
'Pioneer Peggy'

Boeing B-29 "Super Fortress"
'Joltin' Josie—The Pacific Pioneer'

North American B-25 "Mitchell" 'Vikin's Vicious Virgin'

Republic P-47 "Thunderbolt"
'Lovely Lillian'

North American B-25 "Mitchell"
'Mitch The Witch'

Consolidated B-24 "Liberator" 'Flak Fled Flapper'

North American B-25 "Mitchell" 'Leroy's Joy'

Consolidated B-24 "Liberator"
'Moonlight Maid'

ELVGREN

FRENCH DRESSING

Consolidated B-24 "Liberator" 'Our Gal'

CLOSE COVER BEFORE STRIKING
LEE'S BAR
44th and Hiway 20
GARDEN CITY
IDAHO
MEET the CROWD
SNOW FUN
MATCH CORP. OF AMERICA • CHICAGO
MADE IN U.S.A.

Boeing B-29 "Super Fortress" 'Lady Be Good'

'Miss B. Haven' bomber jacket

Boeing B-29 "Super Fortress"

Consolidated B-24 "Liberator"

Consolidated B-24 "Liberator" 'My Devotion'

Boeing B-17 "Flying Fortress" 'Twan-n-g-g-g'

FUNNY GIRLS

Pretty-girl cartoons—and pin-ups based around cartoon-style gags—were a real morale booster for G.I.s. Postcards with gag cartoons joined with such military comic strips as "Male Call," "G.I. Joe" and "The Wolf" to entertain our fighting men in a manner sometimes more risqué than might be seen back home.

"SHE LOVES ME, SHE LOVES ME NOT—"
COPYRIGHT 1942 BY AMERICAN ART SERVICE
"—HAVE LANDED, AND HAVE THE SITUATION WELL IN HAND"
COPYRIGHT 1942 BY AMERICAN ART SERVICE
BONG! BONG!
"GUESS WHO?"
THE C.O.'s GOT A NEW PIN-UP GIRL —
CUT ME OUT—PIN ME UP!
SAN FRANCISCO, CALIFORNIA.
HOME
THANK YOU, MR. CENSOR, FOR YOUR AUTOGRAPH!
HOME
WAR
DUTY COMES FIRST!
COPYRIGHT 1942 BY AMERICAN ART SERVICE
SUE
SWEETHEART
ZZZZ
"KISS ME AGAIN, BETTY!"
COPYRIGHT 1942 BY AMERICAN ART SERVICE
"AW, IT WAS NOTHIN'!"

Boeing B-17 "Flying Fortress" 'Fools Rush In'

North American B-25 "Mitchell" 'Sunday Punch'

Consolidated B-24 "Liberator" 'Cocktail Hour'

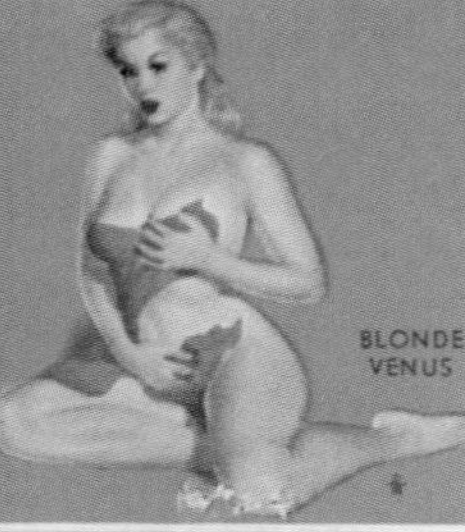

Martin Marauder B-26 'Hard to Get'

Boeing B-29 "Super Fortress"
'Peace on Earth'

Boeing B-29 "Super Fortress"
'Short Time Only'

Boeing B-17 "Flying Fortress"
'Mason and Dixon'

North American P-51 Mustang
'My Achin' Back'

Martin Marauder B-26 'You've 'Ad It'

North American B-25 "Mitchell"
'Oh Dee Whizz'

Boeing B-29 "Super Fortress" 'Tax Exempt'

Consolidated B-24 "Liberator"
'Night and Day'

Boeing B-29 "Super Fortress"
'Lassie, Come Home'

ARTIST'S SKETCH
By Munson
The Jug's Up, Brother
Is my turban disturbin'?
come on you sunners!
Jantzen
AMERICA'S SWIM SUIT
TO BE FREE TO ENJOY TOMORROW... BUY MORE BONDS TODAY!
Are you interested in Chinese Figures?
AND I'VE GOT SOMETHING FOR YOU, TOO
Just a case of

Turkey's famous for its hills — and veils
This should improve my circulation
We've got plenty on the bull
What will my mummy think?
Yes — I'm proud of my fancy
You can't beat the
BOBBIES
KEN and TORCHY
Hiway 42
MEMORIAL DRIVE
MANITOWOC, WIS.
FOLLOW the CROWD
HOWDY AMIGO!
SUPERIOR MATCH
CHICAGO
Southern FRIED CHICKEN
"COAST"
WALNUT GROVE
RESTAURANT
Open 6 A.M. to 10 P.M.
BREAKFAST - LUNCH
DINNER
Coast Highway
DANA POINT, CALIF.
SOUTH OF THE BORDER
Monarch Match
San Jose, Calif.

Martin Marauder B-26 'Six Hits and A Miss'

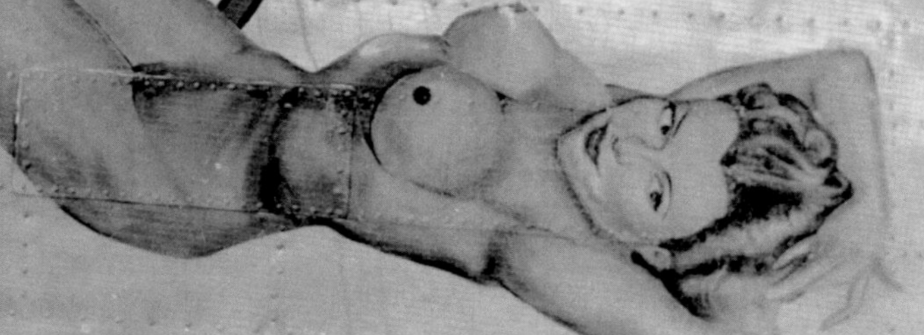

Consolidated B-24 "Liberator" 'Playmate'

Boeing B-29 "Super Fortre
'Sweat'er Out'

Lockheed P-38 Lightning
'Dot–Dash'

Boeing B-29 "Super Fortress"
'There'll Always Be a Christmas'

Boeing B-29 "Super Fortress"
'Miss Hart of America–Holiday Island'

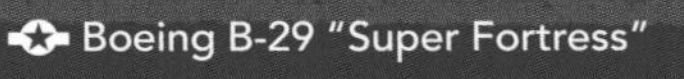

Boeing B-29 "Super Fortress"
'Supine Sue–The International Figure'

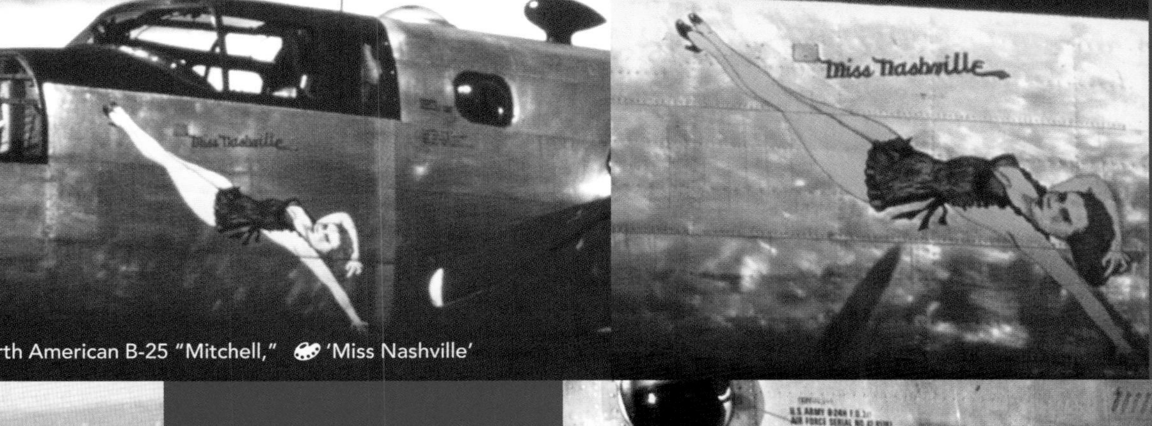

North American B-25 "Mitchell," 'Miss Nashville'

Reading the 'Woonsocket Call' under an Esquire/Vargas calendar is Johnny Godfrey 36 kill ace of the 4th Fighter Group

Consolidated B-24 "Liberator"
'Shoo Shoo Baby'

Martin Marauder B-26

North American B-25 "Mitchell" 'Pin Up Girl'

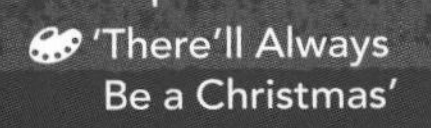

Boeing B-29 "Super Fortress"
'There'll Always Be a Christmas'

Boeing B-17 "Flying Fortress" 'Love !Em! All'

"Things are peaceful here—you'd hardly know there's a war going on… in the evening there is entertainment in the form of conversation, music, baseball and occasional movies."

JUNE 10, 1943

Boeing B-29 "Super Fortress" 'Times A Wastin!'

Republic P-47 "Thunderbolt," 'Red–E–Ruth'

Boeing B-29 "Super Fortress" 'Sleepy Time Gal'

Consolidated B-24 "Liberator" 'Pom Pom Express'

Boeing B-29 "Super Fortress"
'Slick's Chick's'

Boeing B-29 "Super Fortress" 'Lucky Lady'

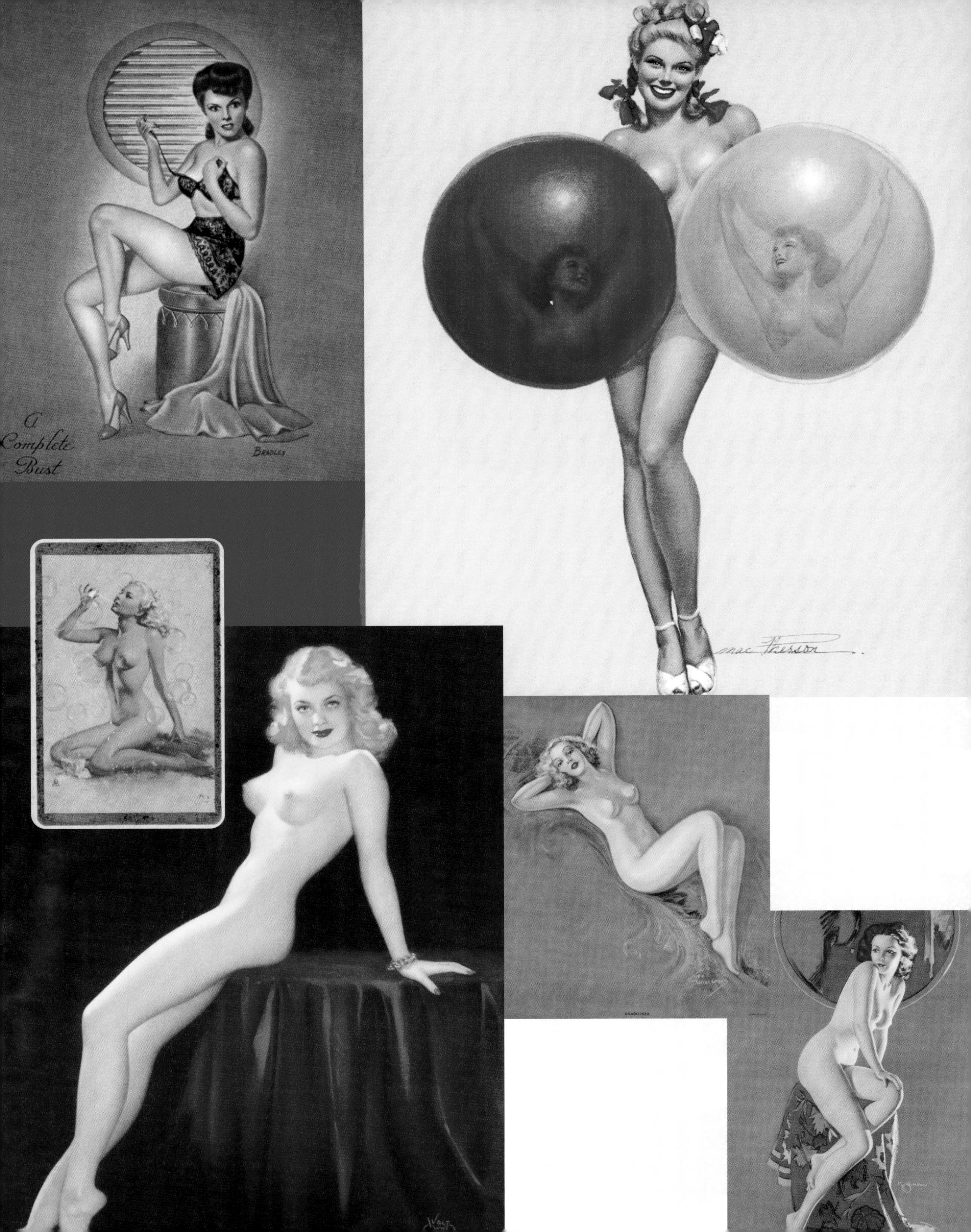
A Complete Bust
BRADLEY
mac Pherson
UNADORNED

NO
STARES!
CRAPO'S
CRAPO'S
GROCERIES
Phone 7025
Open Evenings
Sat. & Sun. Till Midnite
426 E. 4TH
OLYMPIA, WASH
CLOSE COVER FOR SAFETY
NO
STARES!
SUPERIOR MATCH CO., CHICAGO, U.S.A.
ELVGREN

OUT ON A LIMB

49th Fighter Squadron rec hall 14th Ftr. Group North Africa/Algeria location

Inside rec hall, 14th F/G, 49th F/S

Inside of a bunker, nissan hut art 8th AF England

Close-up of nissan hut art

Lamgford Lodge, England

Road sign found somewhere in Saidor, New Guinea, 1944

Lamgford Lodge, England

Lamgford Lodge, England

Boeing B-17 "Flying Fortress" Untitled

A Life Saver
LIFE GUARD
"WHERE QUALITY IS NOT EXPENSIVE"
GAspee 1-4023
PROVIDENCE, R. I.
"WHERE QUALITY IS NOT EXPENSIVE"
PROVIDENCE, R. I.
Up and Cunning
"WHERE QUALITY IS NOT EXPENSIVE"
FEDERAL PRESS Inc.
Printers and Lithographers
GAspee 1-4023
179 ATWELLS AVENUE
PROVIDENCE, R. I.
Inflation Control
FEDERAL
179 ATWELLS AVENUE

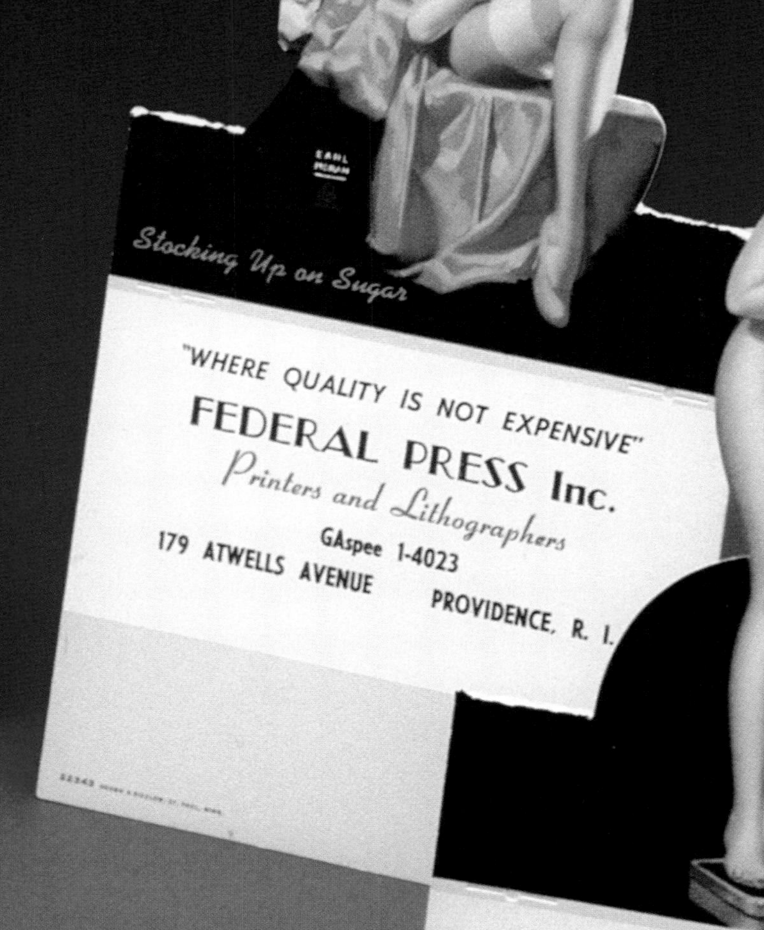

STANDING AT ATTENTION

The pop-up pretties are all the work of legendary pin-up artist Earl Moran, whose pastel pin-ups were among the most popular of the 20th Century. Today Moran is perhaps most famous for having used Marilyn Monroe—prior to her fame—as a frequent model.

Puts A
PLANE
in the
SKY
Buy WAR
TWENTY COMPLETE STORIES FOR FIVE CENTS
Hollywood
HOLLYWOOD
5¢
SEPTEMBER
ACTORS ARE CATTLE!
SAYS DIRECTOR ALFRED HITCHCOCK
Going My Way
EARL MORAN
VISIBILITY PERFECT

Keaton's
KITCHEN
1212 S. W. 3rd
Portland, Oregon
The HOT Spot
National Press, Chicago
"HE'S TAKEN A TURN
FOR THE NURSE"

Lamgford Lodge, England

Lamgford Lodge, England

Boeing B-29 "Super Fortress"
'Thunderhead'

Boeing B-17 "Flying Fortress" 'D-Day Doll'

Consolidated B-24 "Liberator"
'Atomic Blonde'

Republic P-47 "Thunderbolt"
'Honolulu Tina'

Boeing B-29 "Super Fortress"
'Inspiration'

Boeing B-29 "Super Fortress"
'Joker's Wild'

Boeing B-29 "Super Fortress"
'Joker's Wild II'

Boeing B-29 "Super Fortress"
'Jack Pot'

Consolidated B-24 "Liberator"
'Gambler's Luck'

Boeing B-29 "Super Fortress" 'Lucky 'Leven'

Boeing B-29 "Super Fortress"
'Lucky Irish'

HIGH AND DRY
Gunnison's
GRILL
318 S. E.
GRAND AVE.
VE 9224
MATCH CORP. OF AMERICA • CHICAGO
MADE IN U.S.A.
WELL EQUIPPED
WELL EQUIPPED
V---MAIL
UNITED STATES
Official
V MAIL
LETTER-SHEET ENVELOPES
FOR RUSH PHOTOGRAPHIC MAIL TO OUR ARMED FORCES OVERSEAS
INSTRUCTIONS
HOLD EVERYTHING
NO SWIMMING ALLOWED
"Thinking of You"
STATIONERY KIT
WHAT EVERY SERVICEMAN NEEDS FOR HIS WRITING PLEASURE
VIA AIR MAIL

"Every new thing that I do somehow makes me think of you. Every path, though strange and far, leads my heart to where you are. And the only road for me is with you across the sea."

AUGUST 30, 1945

Boeing B-29 "Super Fortress" 'Sky Queen'

Boeing B-17 "Flying Fortress"

Consolidated B-24 "Liberator" 'Black M'

Consolidated B-24 "Liberator" Undecided'

Shape Ahoy
"WHERE THE CUSTOMER IS ALWAYS WRONG"
THE GYPSY
610-12 N.W. 21st Av.
PORTLAND, ORE.
Phone BR. 4902
A SAILOR'S DREAM
LET'S GO U.S.A.
KEEP 'EM ROLLING

EARL MORAN

MonarchMatch's
San Jose, Calif.
Always a friendly WELCOME
Maid to Order!
ROBBINS INN
Lois & Jack Downing
Phone MU. 9651
3000
N. Commercial Ave.
Portland 12, Oregon

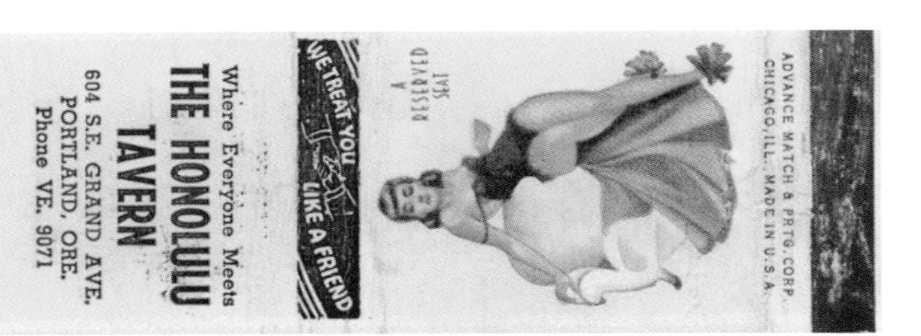
ADVANCE MATCH & PRTG. CORP.
CHICAGO, ILL. MADE IN U.S.A.
WE TREAT YOU LIKE A FRIEND
Where Everyone Meets
THE HONOLULU TAVERN
604 S.E. GRAND AVE.
PORTLAND, ORE.
Phone VE. 9071

RED FOR COURAGE
WHITE FOR HONOR
BLUE FOR JUSTICE

MATCH CORP. OF AMERICA - CHICAGO
MADE IN U.S.A.
GLOVELY
SERVICE WITH A SMILE
EKMAN & CO.
AUTO PARTS &
MACHINE SHOP
1626 N. E. UNION AVE.
Phone MU 2155

SAN JOSE, CAL.
SAILOR, BEWARE!
SERVICE With a Smile
JACK'S
FLYING A SERVICE
13406 HWY. 99
VANCOUVER, WASH.
Phone OX. 3-2456
Close Cover For Safety

National Press, Chicago
GOOD PICKIN'S
Phone EX. 9591
THE CAMEL
CLUB
SAILOR'S HAVEN
1034 KEARNY ST.
JUST UP THE HUMP
FROM INT. SETTLEMENT
San Francisco, Calif.
CLOSE COVER FOR SAFETY

MATCH CORP. OF AMERICA • CHICAGO
CLEAN SWEEP
PARKING
OASIS
CLUB
COCKTAILS
DANCING
BURLEY, IDAHO
CLOSE COVER BEFORE STRIKING

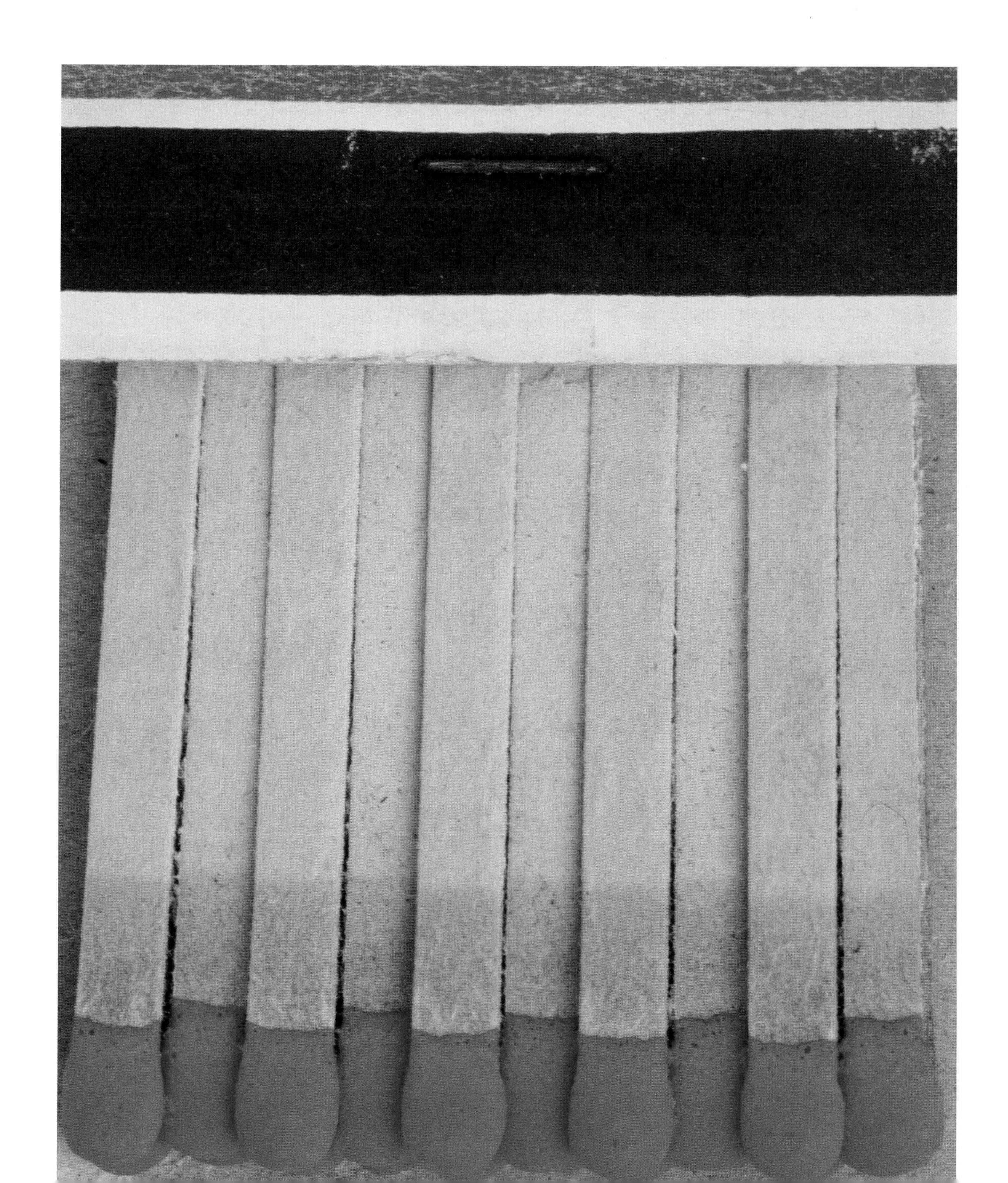

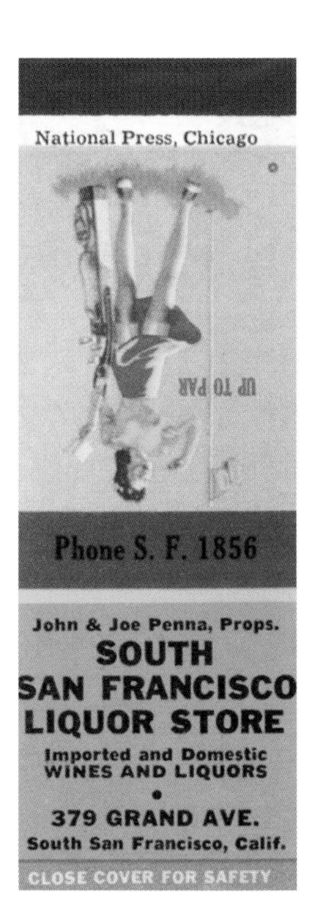
National Press, Chicago
UP TO PAR
Phone S. F. 1856
John & Joe Penna, Props.
SOUTH
SAN FRANCISCO
LIQUOR STORE
Imported and Domestic
WINES AND LIQUORS
379 GRAND AVE.
South San Francisco, Calif.
CLOSE COVER FOR SAFETY

MATCH CORP. OF AMERICA • CHICAGO
MADE IN U.S.A.
JUST RIGHT
NO JOB
TOO LARGE
OR TOO SMALL
A.A.A.A.
FIRE EXTINGUISHER
SERVICE
1301 S. W. 1st AVE.
PORTLAND 1, ORE.
CLOSE COVER BEFORE STRIKING

Boeing B-17 "Flying Fortress" 'Extra Special'

NEWS FROM FRONT

Boeing B-29 "Super Fortress" 'Dina Might'

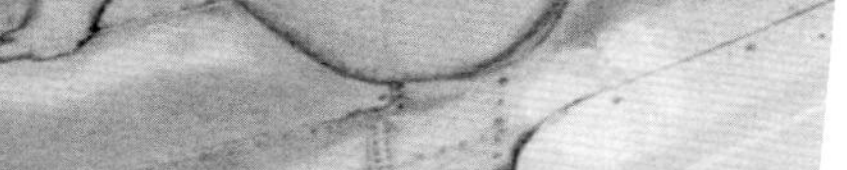
Douglas C-47 Dakota 'Cherie'

Republic P-47 "Thunderbolt" 'Betty Lou'

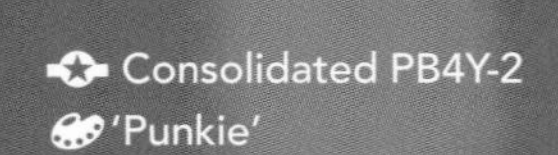
Consolidated PB4Y-2
'Punkie'

Consolidated B-24 "Liberator" 'Glamouras'

Republic P-47 "Thunderbolt" 'Kandy K II'

Consolidated B-24 "Liberator" 'Daisy Mae'

Republic P-47 "Thunderbolt" 'Gloria'

Boeing B-29 "Super Fortress" 'Doris Anne'

HELLO—HOW DO YOU LIKE MY LINES?
YOU ARE ALWAYS WELCOME
JACK POT CAFE
Cold Beer
Al & Eunice Gamble Props.
Phone 9181
FARMINGTON, CALIF.
IN PERFECT SHAPE!
HERE I AM!
SORRY I HAD TO LEAVE
"BEAU"
FAN MAIL for
SHORT ORDERS
COLD BEER
AND
FOUNTAIN
RALPH & KATHLEEN REASONER
Delicious
SHORT AND SWEET!
WHY HUG THE SHOR
WHEN I'M AROUND
WAITING FOR MY "MALE"!

NATURE'S
ONDERFUL!
H.M.S EXCELLENT
PLAYER'S
NAVY CUT
Player's
Please
PERSONALITY
PLUS!
B. Armstrong
HAPPY
DAZE!
WHAT'S ON YOUR MIND?
"KNOTTY"
BUT NICE!

THIS POSTER IS PUBLISHED BY THE HOUSE OF SEAGRAM AS PART OF ITS CONTRIBUTION TO THE NATIONAL VICTORY EFFORT

STAMPING OUT THE ENEMY

Even when pretty girls sat on the sidelines, the war effort required bold, cartoony imagery, as demonstrated by these dramatic stamps, which utilize a striking style right out of the comic books

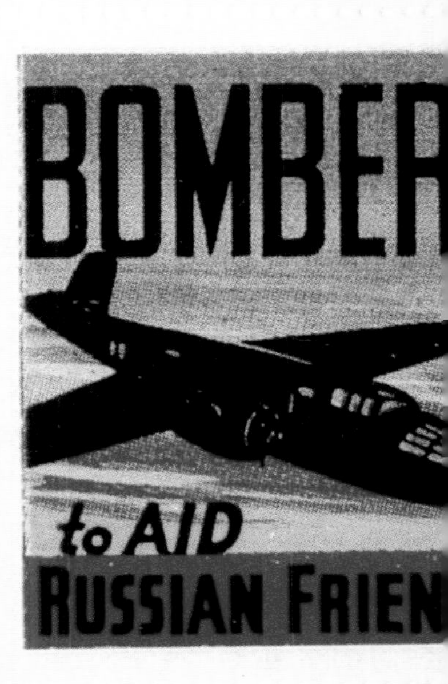

SHED BY THE CZECHOSLOVAK RELIEF CENTRAL COMMITTEE TO COMMEMORATE THE DEDICATION OF AMERICAN "LID

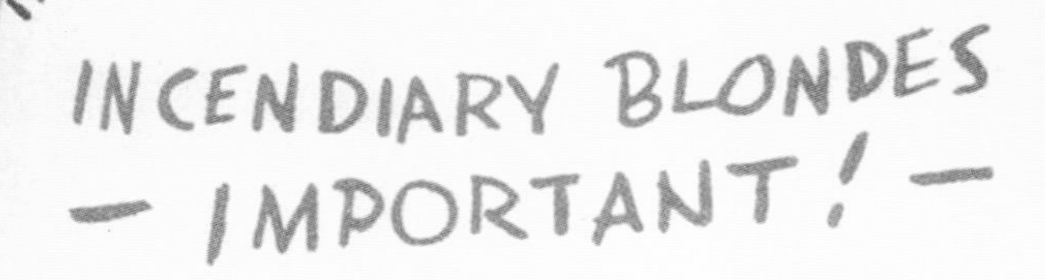

Boeing B-17 "Flying Fortress"
'Incendiary Blonde'

North American B-25 "Mitchell"
'Incendiary Blonde'

"This is IT"

Boeing B-29 "Super Fortress" "This is IT!"

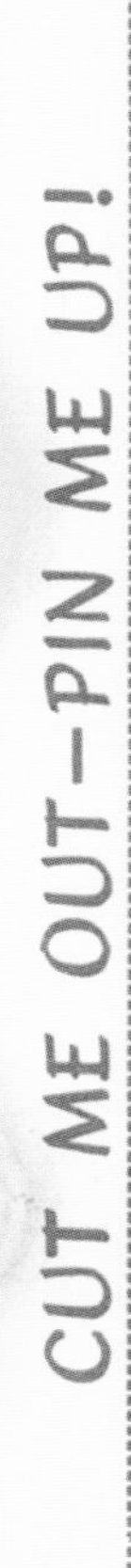

Consolidated B-24 "Liberator" 'Texas Kate'

Painter painting cowgirl is from 79th Ftr. Group in Tunisia

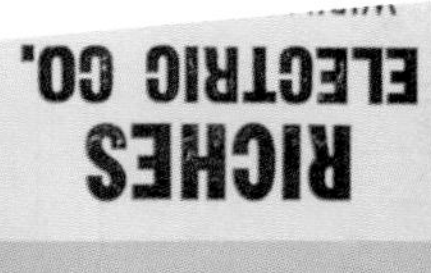

Boeing B-29 "Super Fortress" 'Lady Mary Anna'

Consolidated B-24 "Liberator" 'Missouri Miss'

Boeing B-29 "Super Fortress" 'Lady Mary Anna'

Boeing B-29 "Super Fortress" 'Lady Mary Anna'

"I hope it is soon when I can be home…I hope mom is well and doesn't worry too much. I often dream of coming home and surprising her."

SEPTEMBER 27, 1944

Yes! Uncle Sam_
WE'RE HELPING TO WIN
by
PREVENTING
ACCIDENTS
STONEHOUSE SIGNS FOR ACCIDENT PREVENTION • DENVER
"Signs Since 1862"
Double Trouble
THREE POINT LANDING
ROMANCE
JACK'S
TAVERN
CLOSE COVER FOR SAFETY
JACK & JANE'S
NITE HAWK
BAR-B-Q
BAR-B-Q SPARERIBS
BAR-B-Q PO'KE CHOPS
6423 N. Interstate
PORTLAND, OREGON
MU. 9892
Just a Little
DIFFERENT
WHAT
HO!
SUPERIOR MATCH CO., CHICAGO, U.S.A.
ELVGREN
WHAT HOE!

SUPERIOR MATCH CO., CHICAGO, U.S.A.
19
BELLE RINGER
The Right Place
DRIVE
DELI
BEER Liquors WINES
PHONE 845
Tony Villocco, Prop.
401 E. MAIN ST.
COLLINSVILLE, ILL.
ELVGREN
Belle Ringer

TIME
has been flying,
the YEAR'S
making
TRACKS
But NOW
there's a moment
TO KNOCK OFF
and
RELAX
COME ON ALONG
So let's make the most of it-
You'll see
when
you've tried
You can make
A GOOD START
IF you put
care aside
If you feel
that your CHORES
are a web
to ENMESH YOU,
Slip out
of ROUTINE-
A CHANGE
will refresh
you

BEAUTIFUL CARD

K.O. Munson—known for his "sketchbook" pin-ups—created a number of lovely cards that included mutliple images, increasingly racy as the card opened up to a precursor of the PLAYBOY centerfold.

Consolidated B-24 "Liberator" 'Going My Way'

KNEEDING A LIFT

ELVGREN

Caught in the Draft

Consolidated B-24 "Liberator"
'Puddle Jumper II'

Consolidated B-24 "Liberator" 'Wedding Belle'

Boeing B-29 "Super Fortress" 'The Lady is Fresh'

Consolidated B-24 "Liberator" 'Golden Lady'

Consolidated B-24 "Liberator" 'Milady'

Boeing B-29 "Super Fortress" 'Lady Frances

Boeing B-29 "Super Fortress"
'Liberty Belle'

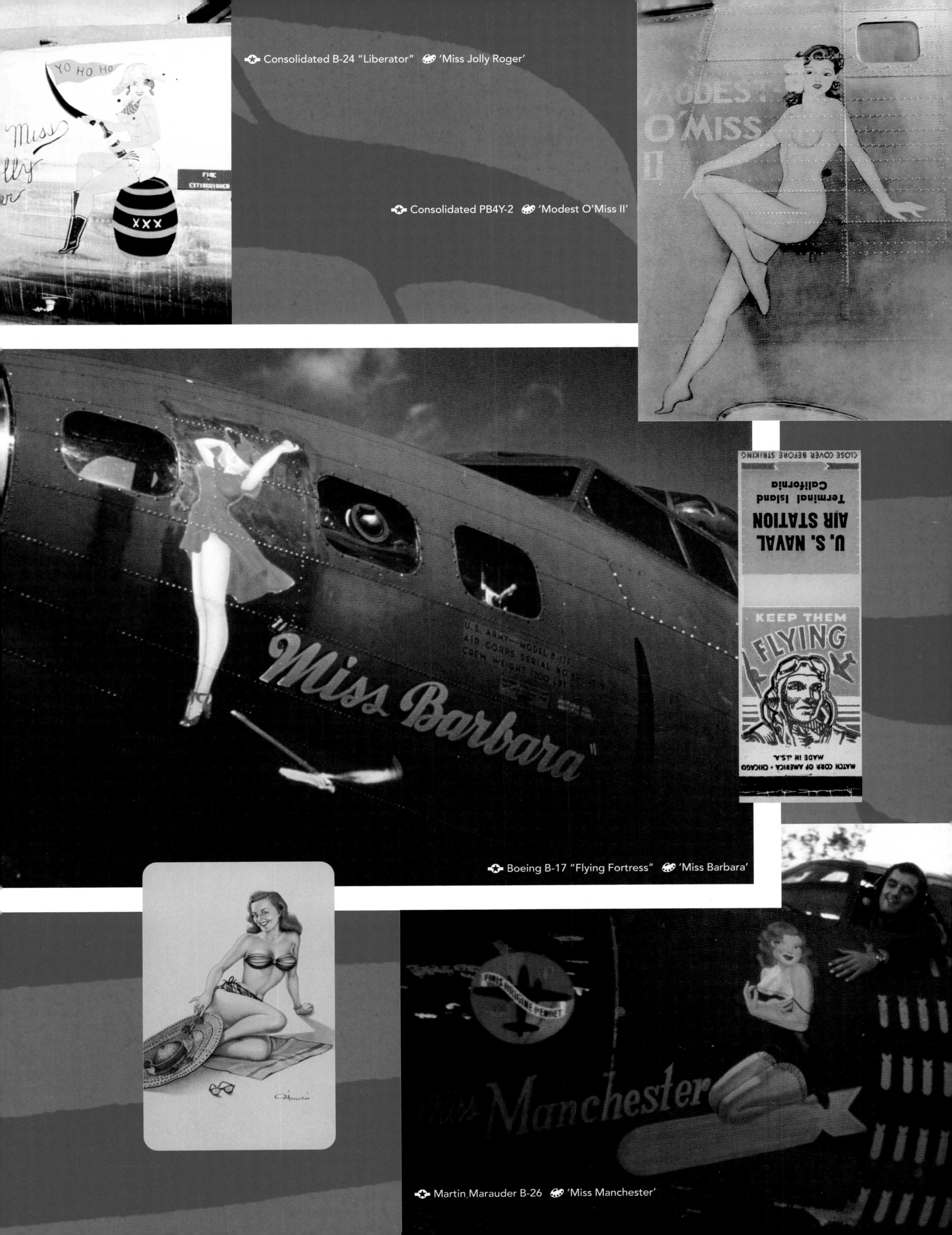

Consolidated B-24 "Liberator" 'Miss Jolly Roger'

Consolidated PB4Y-2 'Modest O'Miss II'

Boeing B-17 "Flying Fortress" 'Miss Barbara'

Martin Marauder B-26 'Miss Manchester'

Open Till 4 A.M.
Biggest Trading Post
In Town
CITY
GROCERY
1735 S.W. Broadway
Portland 1, Ore.
CA. 7-0818
PRESSING
NEED
ELVGREN
IN THE DOUGH
JUST THE TYPE
ELVGREN
SITTING PRETTY

"JUTHT MY THIZE!"
Try Our FOUNTAIN
BERRY BROS.
LUNCH AND
GROCERY
509 N.W. 16TH AVE.
PORTLAND, ORE.
Light Lunches
"JUTHT MY THIZE!"
SUPERIOR MATCH CO., CHICAGO, U.S.A.

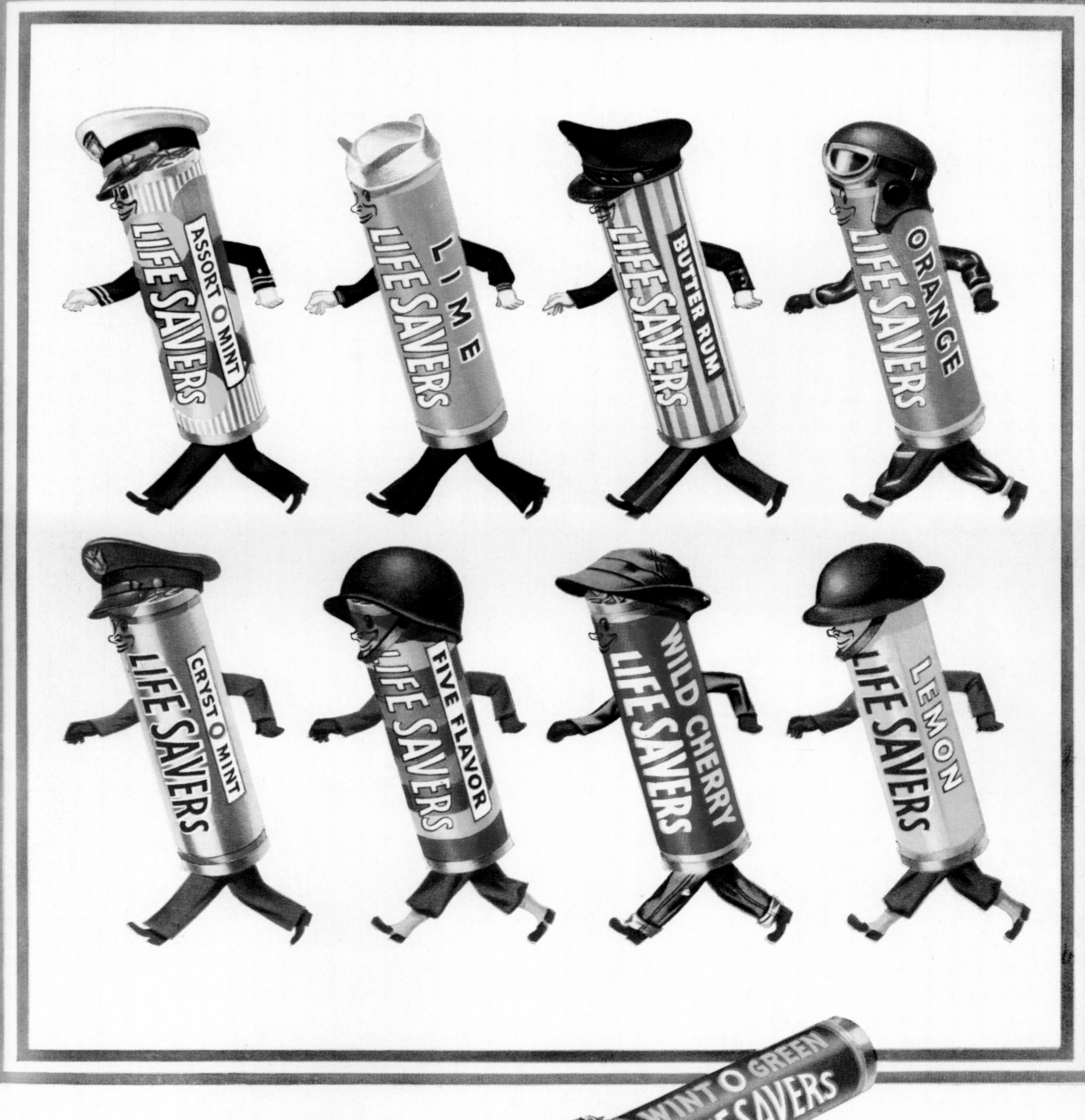

TODAY our armed forces are ordering more and more LIFE SAVERS hard candy for shipment out to CENSORED, CENSORED and CENSORED

So...if you have trouble getting some favorite flavor ...you will know that some soldier, sailor, or marine is enjoying it somewhere, someplace.

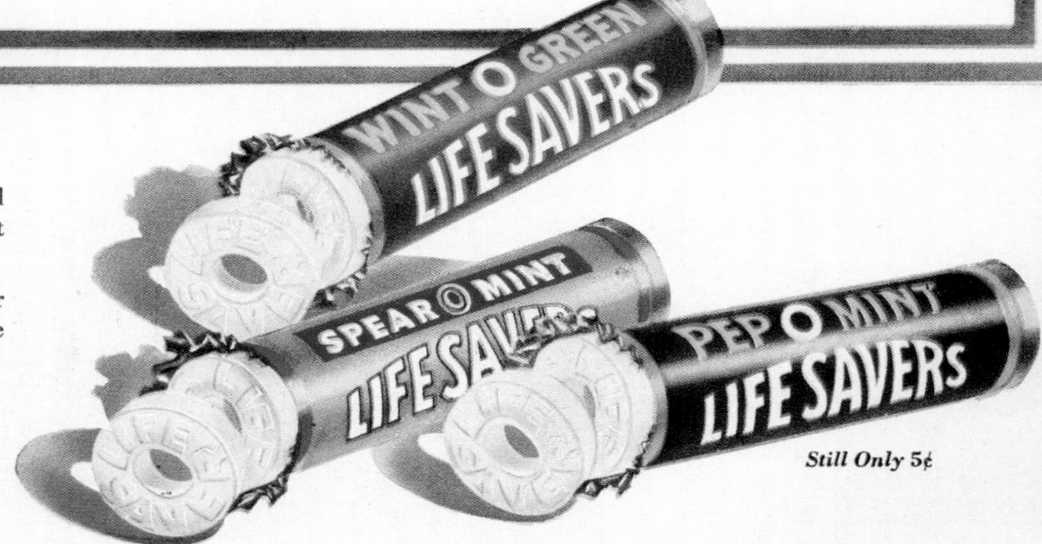

Still Only 5¢

Lockheed P-38 Lightning 'Hawkeye Hattie - II'

North American P-51 Mustang 'Gypsy'

Boeing B-29 "Super Fortress" 'The Heat's On'

Northrop P-61 "Black Widow" 'Midnight Belle'

North American B-25 "Mitchell" 'A Bit of Lace'

Consolidated B-24 "Liberator" 'Squeeze'

North American B-25 "Mitchell" 'Double Trouble'

Douglas C-47 Dakota
'Saylor's Trailer'

Republic P-47 "Thunderbolt" 'Lovely Leo'

Boeing B-29 "Super Fortress"
'The Wichita Witch'

North American B-25 "Mitchell" 'Bundle Bunny'

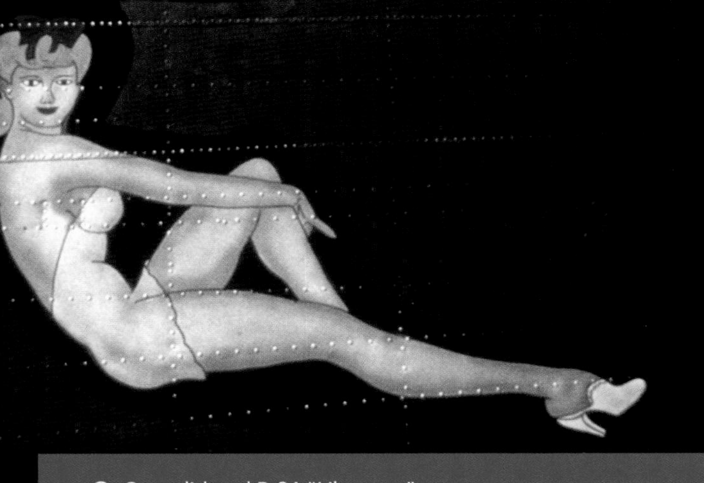

Consolidated B-24 "Liberator"
'Sweet Sixteen'

Boeing B-17 "Flying Fortress" 'Looky Looky'

Republic P-47 "Thunderbolt" 'Stanley's Steamer'

Consolidated B-24 "Liberator" 'Bachelor's Brothel'

THINK I'D BE I-A IN THE ARMY?
ARTIST'S SKETCH PAD
by
EARL MAC PHER
KEEP YOUR
HANDS UP
STRANGER!
HERE'S
A
DATE!
FOR
YOU.
APRIL
1
NO FOOLIN'
THIS END UP
HANDLE
WITH CARE
SPRINGTIME IS SPRINGTIME!
AUG

ARE YOU IN FAVOR
OF THIS MOTION?
NOW - WHAT IS THE NEXT STEP?
HOW DOES IT LOOK
IF I HOLD IT UP LIKE THIS?
RICHARD'S
RESTAURANT
Open Seven Days
4620 S.E. Hawthorne
PORTLAND, ORE.
PHONE VE. 9854
The Right Place
A GOOD
TIE-UP
MONARCH MATCH CO., SAN JOSE, CALIF.
HOW DO YOU LIK
MY TECHNIQUE
I'M HAVING
TROUBLES
WITH MY BUBBLES
I'LL DO MY BESTA FOR THE FIESTA

'Texas Sweetheart' bomber jacket

'Texas Sweetheart' bomber jacket

'Dame Satan' bomber jacket

'Diabolical Angel' bomber jacket, Pacific Theater

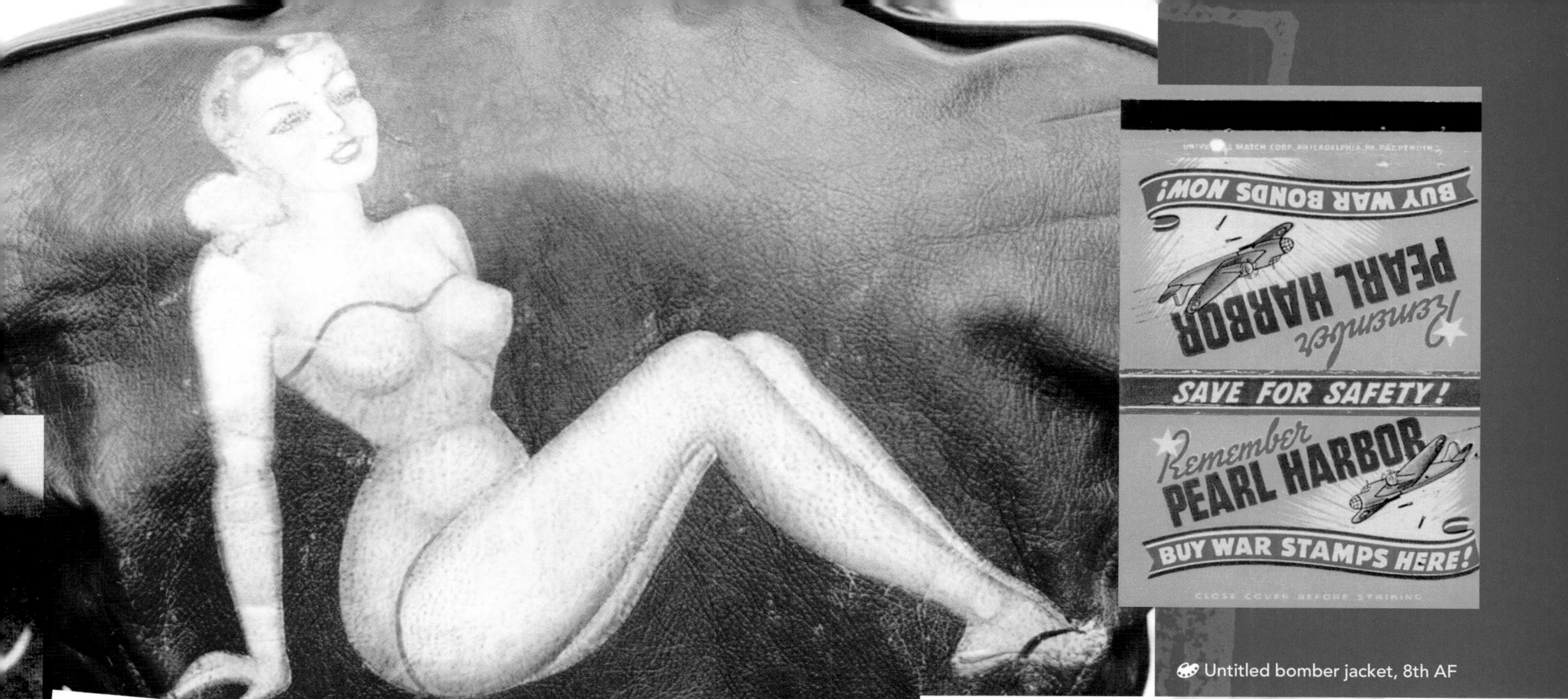

Untitled bomber jacket, 8th AF

'Rosie's Sweat Box' bomber jacket, B-17, 614th B/S, 401st B/G

Consolidated B-24 "Liberator" 'Sweet Routine'

Martin Marauder B-26 'Valkyrie'

Boeing B-17 "Flying Fortress" 'Queenie'

'My Baby' bomber jacket, Maj. Lonnie Eatleston, 11th B/G, 98th B/S

Republic P-47 "Thunderbolt" 'X-L-Ent'

Consolidated B-24 "Liberator" 'Million $ Baby'

Consolidated B-24 "Liberator" 'Shady Lady'

“In the evening the orchestra gets together on the main deck and plays...the boys are still talking about them and probably will for some time to come.”

MARCH 11, 1945

Weekly Pin-up: Newsweek Special for the Armed Forces
She sings. Blond Martha Tilton, formerly with the Benny Goodman band, warbles on the Milton Berle radio show.
May 14, 1945
MOVIES
Bustle, Wit, and Rioting
The Invisible Mr. Rose
Love in 48 Hours
Romance Deferred
Weekly Pin-up: Newsweek Special for the Armed Forces
Yvonne De Carlo, star of Salome—Where She Danced, minus the traditional seven veils
As Thou
Not Sane
Weekly Pin-up: Newsweek Special for the Armed Forces
Cobra-ish: That's how pin-up girl Lynn Baggett, currently appearing in "The Adventures of Mark Twain," looks to servicemen
Two-Star Flier
MOVIES
March Twain

Weekly Pin-up: Newsweek Special for the Armed Forces

NOVEMBER 5, 1945

MOVIES

They Were Real People

It's as unusual to find Jane Russell out of a strawstack as a needle in...

Peck, with eyes and razor; Bergman, ...

Weekly Pin-up: Newsweek Special for the Armed Forces

OCTOBER 22, 1945

MUSIC

35

HAY STACKED

Jane Russell—fresh from a photo shoot for the outrageous Howard Hughes western, "The Outlaw"—and Yvonne DeCarlo—straight from the Florentine Gardens nightclub in Hollywood, and years away from Lily Munster-dom—are just two of the typical beauties in these WW II photographic pin-ups. Pin-up girls could be famous actresses or starlets or even strippers—the boys overseas did not care.

Consolidated B-24 "Liberator" 'Hell's Belle'

Republic P-47 "Thunderbolt" 'Carolina Sunshine'

BAD NEWS,
GOOD NEWS,
COME WHAT MAY
WE'LL ALWAYS
BELIEVE IN THE
U.S.A.
THE CAPTAIN SAYS - YOUNG MA
YOU'RE NOT TAKING
THE NAVY SERIOUSLY

SUNSET
INN
Beer & Wine
HAMBURGERS
Phone 101-J-3
SHASTA DAM BLVD.
Central Valley, Calif.
A
BATON
BEAUTY
EARL
MORAN

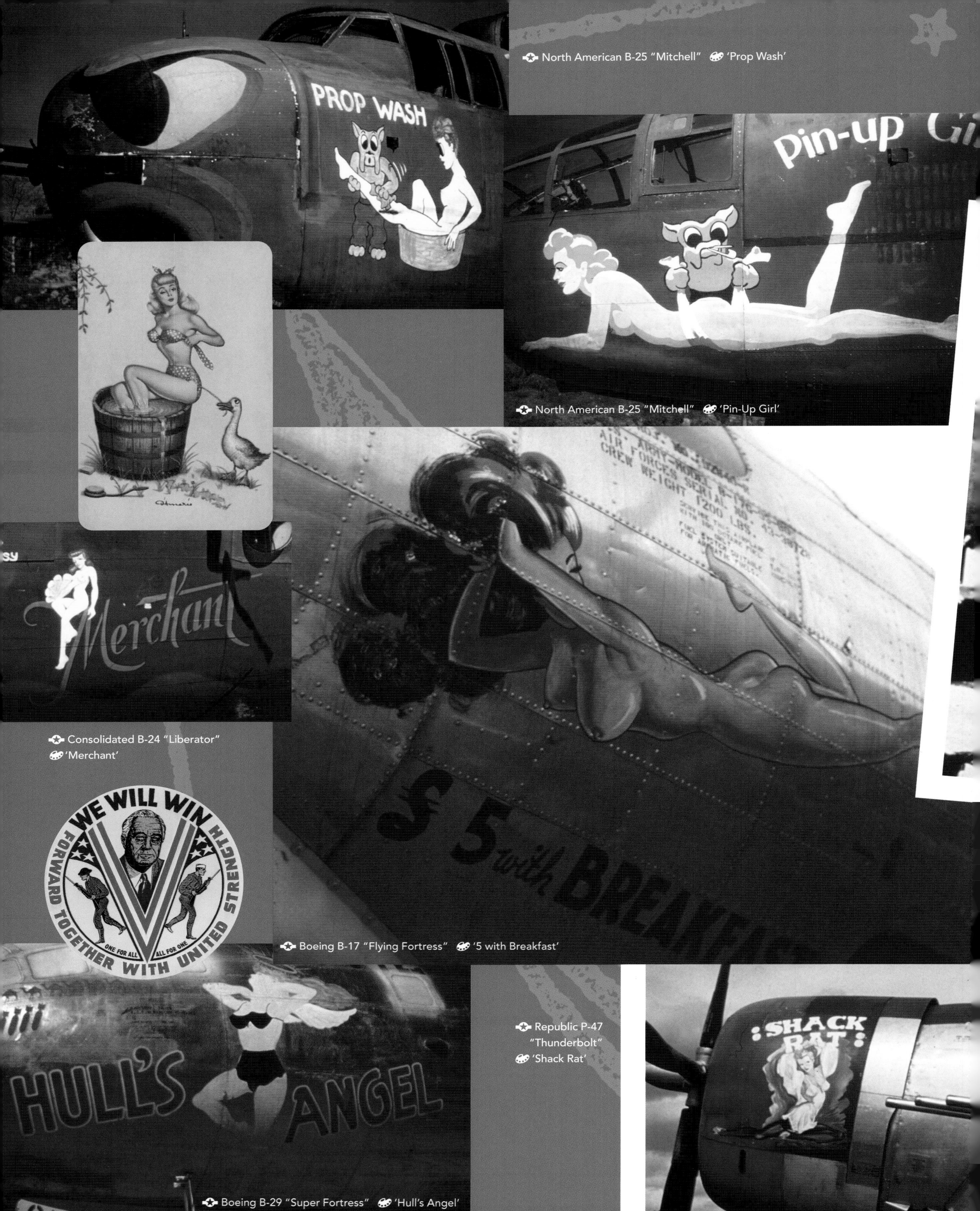

North American B-25 "Mitchell" 'Prop Wash'

North American B-25 "Mitchell" 'Pin-Up Girl'

Consolidated B-24 "Liberator" 'Merchant'

Boeing B-17 "Flying Fortress" '5 with Breakfast'

Republic P-47 "Thunderbolt" 'Shack Rat'

Boeing B-29 "Super Fortress" 'Hull's Angel'

Boeing B-29 "Super Fortress" '20th Century Sweetheart'

Boeing B-17 "Flying Fortress" 'Chatterbox'

Boeing B-17 "Flying Fortress" 'Sweet and Lovely'

Consolidated B-24 "Liberator" 'Wistful Vista'

Boeing B-29 "Super Fortress" 'Three Feathers'

'Star Dust' bomber jacket, 494th B/G, 867th B/S

EXTRA | PARIS EDITION | EXTRA

THE STARS AND STRIPES

Daily Newspaper of U.S. Armed Forces in the European Theater of Operations

Vol. 1—No. 285 * 1 Fr. 1 Fr. Tuesday, May 8, 1945

VICTORY

Nazis Reveal Surrender To Western Allies, Russia

The unconditional surrender of Germany to the Western Allies and Soviet Russia was announced by the German high command yesterday morning.

The official announcements from the Allied governments are expected to come simultaneously from Washington, London and Moscow today.

nouncement at 3 PM.

President Truman said he had agreed with the British and Russian governments that no surrender proclamation would be made 'until simultaneous announcements could be made by the three governments.'

King George VI of England sent Gen. Eisenhower a cablegram last night congratulating him and his armies on the 'complete and crushing victory' in Europe.

The Associated Press broke the news of the surrender in a story from Rheims, France, that the Allies had announced Germany's surrender at 0241 hours yesterday morning. It said the surrender took place in the little red school house that is Gen. Eisenhower's headquarters.

Col. Gen. Gustaf Jodl, German army chief of staff, signed for Germany, it was reported.

The Associated Press story apparently was premature. From dispatches coming from Washington and London, it appeared that arrangements were being made to announce the surrender simultaneously in the three capitals when the news broke. This seemed apparent from President Truman's statement and news stories from London saying that Truman, Churchill and Stalin had conferred by telephone during the day.

Supreme Headquarters said it authorized no such story to be sent out. However, the American Broadcasting Station in Europe—operated by the Office of War Information—was reported by International News Service to have

(Continued on Page 8)

Nazis Still Fight Reds At Prague

Russian and U.S. Third Army troops, despite Germany's reported unconditional surrender, continued their sweep into Czechoslovakia yesterday after the Nazi commander there announced his forces still were at war with Russia.

Gen. Patton's famous Fourth Armored Div. last night was reported speeding toward Prague, where partisans and Germans were locked in a struggle for control of the capital. A Czech radio broadcast said Gen. Patton's troops were only 15 miles away and London reports said it was "entirely possible" that American vanguards already were in the city.

Russians Capture Breslau

Enemy sources said Marshal Ivan Koniev's First Ukrainian Army had entered Bohemia from Saxony at a point probably 60 to 65 miles north of Prague.

All fighting stopped yesterday in Breslau, the Silesian capital which has been a battleground since Feb. 17. Marshal Stalin in an order of

(Continued on Page 2)

Prayer, Tears, Laughter —The World Celebrates

By David A. Gordon
Stars and Stripes Staff Writer

People in Allied cities throughout the world yesterday accepted the news of the reported unconditional surrender of Germany as true—despite lack of official announcements from the governments of the U.S., Britain and Russia—and celebrated with prayer, liquor, tears and laughter.

Crowds milled in the streets of the world's great cities—in Times Square, New York; Trafalgar Square and Piccadilly Circus in London, and along the Champs-Elysées, Paris—but it was not a wild jubilee. The absence of a clear-cut official announcement and the piece-by-piece collapse of the German Armies tended to dull the feeling of triumph.

Ticker Tape Showers Wall Street

Then, too, the huge casualty lists, the vast war against Japan that still lay ahead, the levelled cities and the shell-pitted fields and the absence of sons, fathers and brothers from homes, checked unrestrained exuberance.

Ticker tape poured from the office windows of Wall Street and shreds of telephone books from the windows of the Garment Center buildings in the Thirties, and men and women flooded Times Square, waving their arms and trying to express in words their happiness. Liquor, flowed inside bars, while people held newspaper extras and devoured the news.

Orderly Celebration Makes Things Easy for Police

But there was no special need for strict police measures, because the celebrating was orderly. Aristocratic Fifth Avenue in New York City also was covered with ripped sheets of paper which became shapeless messes in the wet streets, but stores remained open and some people seemed more dazed than jubilant.

On one section of Fifth Avenue, an impromptu conga line was formed, and on another, a group of girls marched spontane-

(Continued on Page 8)

Tail Wind
ELVGREN
© LITHO U.S.A.

North American B-25 "Mitchell" 'Miss-Behavin'

Boeing B-29 "Super Fortress" 'Tail Wind'

THANK YOU GIRLS

Nothing could light up the face of a pilot or sailor or soldier more readily than a beautiful girl from back home. In the demanding, lonely, dangerous world of the overseas military man, pin-up girls promised a better life awaited them, stateside—when the war could fade from grim reality to bittersweet nostalgia.